RichDad Series

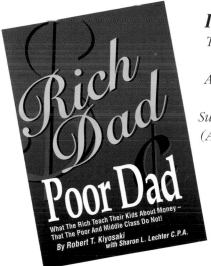

Featured on the bestseller lists of:

The New York Times, The Wall Street Journal, USA Today, Business Week, Amazon.com, Amazon.com UK and Germany, E-trade.com, Sydney Morning Herald (Australia), Sun Herald (Australia), Business Review Weekly (Australia), Borders Books and Music (U.S. and Singapore), Barnes & Noble.com

Featured on the bestseller lists of:

Sydney Morning Herald (Australia), Sun Herald (Australia), Business Review Weekly (Australia), Amazon.com, Barnes & Noble.com, Borders Books and Music (U.S. and Singapore),

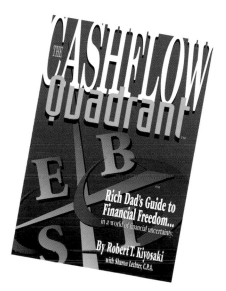

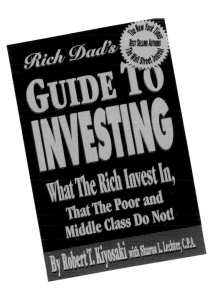

The next Rich Dad bestseller:

To be released in Summer of 2000

"To get over the top financially, you must read *Rich Dad Poor Dad*. It's common sense and market savvy for your financial future."

Zig Ziglar
World-renowned author and lecturer

"If you want all insider wisdom on how to personally get and STAY rich, read this book! Bribe your kids (financially if you have to) to do the same."

Mark Victor Hansen
Co-author, New York Times
#1 Best Selling *Chicken Soup for the Soul*® *series*

"Rich Dad Poor Dad is not your usual book on money...*Rich Dad Poor Dad* is easy to read and its key messages — such as, getting rich takes focus and nerve, are very simple."

Honolulu Magazine

"I only wish I had read this book when I was young, or even better yet my parents had read this book! This is the kind of book you buy and give each of your kids and buy extra copies, on the chance you have grandchildren and this should be your gift, as soon as this child reaches 8 or 9."

Sue Brawn
President of Tenant Chek of America

"Rich Dad Poor Dad is not about getting rich quickly. It is about taking responsibility for your financial affairs and improving wealth by mastering money. Read it if you want to awaken your financial genius."

Dr. Ed Koken
Lecturer on Finance,
RMIT University, Melbourne

"I wish I would have read this book twenty years ago."

Larison Clark, Diamond Key Homes
INC. Magazine's Fastest Growing Home
Builder in America, 1995

"Rich Dad Poor Dad is a starting point for anyone looking to gain control of their financial future."

USA TODAY

Rich Dad,
Poor Dad

What The Rich Teach Their Kids About Money— That The Poor And Middle Class Do Not!

By Robert T. Kiyosaki
with Sharon L. Lechter C.P.A.

Published by
TechPress, Inc.
P.O. Box 5870
Scottsdale, Arizona 85261 U.S.A.
480-998-6971

Kiyosaki, Robert T. and Lechter, Sharon L.
Rich Dad Poor Dad: what the rich teach their kids about money that the poor and middle class do not/Robert T. Kiyosaki with Sharon L. Lechter
p. cm.
ISBN 0-9643856-1-9 Pbk.
1. Personal Finance 2. Business Education 3. Success - Financial
4. Investments I. Title

Designed by Insync Graphic Studio, Inc.
Printed in the United States of America
CTIIGSOPC/1199-9 8 7 6 5

BOOK DEDICATION

*This book is dedicated to all parents everywhere,
a child's most important teachers.*

ACKNOWLEDGEMENTS:

*H*ow does a person say "thank you" when there are so many people to thank? Obviously this book is a thank you to my two fathers who were powerful role models, and to my mom who taught me love and kindness.

Yet, the people most directly responsible for this book becoming a reality include my wife Kim who makes my life complete. Kim is my partner in marriage, business, and in life. Without her I would be lost. To Kim's parents, Winnie and Bill Meyer for raising such a great daughter. I thank Sharon Lechter for picking up the pieces of this book in my computer and putting them together. To Sharon's husband Mike for being a great intellectual property attorney, and their children Phillip, Shelly, and Rick for their participation and cooperation. I thank Keith Cunningham for financial wisdom and inspiration; Larry and Lisa Clark for the gift of friendship and encouragement; Rolf Parta for technical genius; Anne Nevin, Bobbi DePorter and Joe Chapon for insights into learning; DC and John Harrison, Jannie Tay, Sandy Khoo, Richard and Veronica Tan, Peter Johnston and Suzi Dafnis, Jacqueline Seow, Nyhl Henson, Michael and Monette Hamlin, Edwin and Camilla Khoo, K.C. See and Jessica See, for professional support; Kevin and Sara of InSync for brilliant graphics; John and Shari Burley, Bill and Cindy Shopoff, Van Tharp, Diane Kennedy, C.W. Allen, Marilu Deignan, Kim Arries, and Tom Weisenborn, for their financial intelligence. Sam Georges, Anthony Robbins, Enid Vien, Lawrence and Jayne Taylor-West, Alan Wright, Zig Ziglar, for mental clarity; J.W. Wilson, Marty Weber, Randy Craft, Don Mueller, Brad Walker, Blair and Eileen Singer, Wayne and Lynn Morgan, Mimi Brennan, Jerome Summers, Dr. Peter Powers, Will Hepburn, Dr. Enrique Teuscher, Dr. Robert Marin, Betty Oyster, Julie Belden, Jamie Danforth, Cherie Clark, Rick Merica, Joia Jitahide, Jeff Bassett, Dr. Tom Burns, and Bill Galvin for being great friends and supporters of the projects; to the Center Managers and the tens of thousands of graduates of Money and You and The Business School for Entrepreneurs; and to Frank Crerie, Clint Miller, Thomas Allen and Norman Long for being great partners in business.

Table of Contents

There is a Need

Does school prepare children for the real world? "Study hard and get good grades and you will find a high-paying job with great benefits," my parents used to say. Their goal in life was to provide a college education for my older sister and me, so that we would have the greatest chance for success in life. When I finally earned my diploma in 1976—graduating with honors, and near the top of my class, in accounting from Florida State University—my parents had realized their goal. It was the crowning achievement of their lives. In accordance with the "Master Plan," I was hired by a "Big 8" accounting firm, and I looked forward to a long career and retirement at an early age.

My husband, Michael, followed a similar path. We both came from hard-working families, of modest means but with strong work ethics. Michael also graduated with honors, but he did it twice: first as an engineer and then from law school. He was quickly recruited by a prestigious Washington, D.C., law firm that specialized in patent law, and his future seemed bright, career path well-defined and early retirement guaranteed.

Although we have been successful in our careers, they have not turned out quite as we expected. We both have changed positions several times—for all the right reasons—but there are no pension plans vesting on our behalf. Our retirement funds are growing only through our individual contributions.

Michael and I have a wonderful marriage with three great children. As I write this, two are in college and one is just beginning high school. We have spent a fortune making sure our children have received the best education available.

One day in 1996, one of my children came home disillusioned with school. He was bored and tired of studying. "Why should I put time into studying subjects I will never use in real life?" he protested.

Without thinking, I responded, "Because if you don't get good grades, you won't get into college."

"Regardless of whether I go to college," he replied, "I'm going to be rich."

"If you don't graduate from college, you won't get a good job," I responded with a tinge of panic and motherly concern. "And if you don't have a good job, how do you plan to get rich?"

My son smirked and slowly shook his head with mild boredom. We have had this talk many times before. He lowered his head and rolled his eyes. My words of motherly wisdom were falling on deaf ears once again.

Though smart and strong-willed, he has always been a polite and respectful young man.

"Mom," he began. It was my turn to be lectured. "Get with the times! Look around; the richest people didn't get rich because of their educations. Look at Michael Jordan and Madonna. Even Bill Gates, who dropped out of Harvard, founded Microsoft; he is now the richest man in America, and he's still in his 30s. There is a baseball pitcher who makes more than $4 million a year even though he has been labeled 'mentally challenged.' "

There was a long silence between us. It was dawning on me that I was giving my son the same advice my parents had given me. The world around us has changed, but the advice hasn't.

Getting a good education and making good grades no longer ensures success, and nobody seems to have noticed, except our children.

"Mom," he continued, "I don't want to work as hard as you and dad do. You make a lot of money, and we live in a huge house with lots of toys. If I follow your advice, I'll wind up like you, working harder and harder only to pay more taxes and wind up in debt. There is no job security anymore; I know all about downsizing and rightsizing. I also know that college graduates today earn less than you did when you graduated. Look at doctors. They don't make nearly as much money as they used to. I know I can't rely on Social Security or company pensions for retirement. I need new answers."

2

He was right. He needed new answers, and so did I. My parents' advice may have worked for people born before 1945, but it may be disastrous for those of us born into a rapidly changing world. No longer can I simply say to my children, "Go to school, get good grades, and look for a safe, secure job."

I knew I had to look for new ways to guide my children's education.

As a mother as well as an accountant, I have been concerned by the lack of financial education our children receive in school. Many of today's youth have credit cards before they leave high school, yet they have never had a course in money or how to invest it, let alone understand how compound interest works on credit cards. Simply put, without financial literacy and the knowledge of how money works, they are not prepared to face the world that awaits them, a world in which spending is emphasized over savings.

When my oldest son became hopelessly in debt with his credit cards as a freshman in college, I not only helped him destroy the credit cards, but I also went in search of a program that would help me educate my children on financial matters.

One day last year, my husband called me from his office. "I have someone I think you should meet," he said. "His name is Robert Kiyosaki. He's a businessman and investor, and he is here applying for a patent on an educational product. I think it's what you have been looking for."

Just What I Was Looking For

My husband, Mike, was so impressed with *CASHFLOW*, the new educational product that Robert Kiyosaki was developing, that he arranged for both of us to participate in a test of the prototype. Because it was an educational game, I also asked my 19-year-old daughter, who was a freshman at a local university, if she would like to take part, and she agreed.

About fifteen people, broken into three groups, participated in the test.

Mike was right. It was the educational product I had been looking for. But it had a twist: It looked like a colorful Monopoly board with a giant well-dressed rat in the middle. Unlike Monopoly, however, there were two tracks: one inside and one outside. The object of the game was to get out of the inside track—what Robert called the "Rat Race"—

and reach the outer track, or the "Fast Track." As Robert put it, the Fast Track simulates how rich people play in real life.

Robert then defined the "Rat Race" for us.

"If you look at the life of the average-educated, hard-working person, there is a similar path. The child is born and goes to school. The proud parents are excited because the child excels, gets fair to good grades, and is accepted into a college. The child graduates, maybe goes on to graduate school and then does exactly as programmed: looks for a safe, secure job or career. The child finds that job, maybe as a doctor or a lawyer, or joins the Army or works for the government. Generally, the child begins to make money, credit cards start to arrive in mass, and the shopping begins, if it already hasn't.

"Having money to burn, the child goes to places where other young people just like them hang out, and they meet people, they date, and sometimes they get married. Life is wonderful now, because today, both men and women work. Two incomes are bliss. They feel successful, their future is bright, and they decide to buy a house, a car, a television, take vacations and have children. The happy bundle arrives. The demand for cash is enormous. The happy couple decides that their careers are vitally important and begin to work harder, seeking promotions and raises. The raises come, and so does another child and the need for a bigger house. They work harder, become better employees, even more dedicated. They go back to school to get more specialized skills so they can earn more money. Maybe they take a second job. Their incomes go up, but so does the tax bracket they're in and the real estate taxes on their new large home, and their Social Security taxes, and all the other taxes. They get their large paycheck and wonder where all the money went. They buy some mutual funds and buy groceries with their credit card. The children reach 5 or 6 years of age, and the need to save for college increases as well as the need to save for their retirement.

"That happy couple, born 35 years ago, is now trapped in the Rat Race for the rest of their working days. They work for the owners of their company, for the government paying taxes, and for the bank paying off a mortgage and credit cards.

"Then, they advise their own children to 'study hard, get good grades, and find a safe job or career.' They learn nothing about money, except from those who profit from their naiveté, and work hard all their lives. The process repeats into another hard-working generation. This is the 'Rat Race'."

The only way to get out of the "Rat Race" is to prove your proficiency at both accounting and investing, arguably two of the most difficult subjects to master. As a trained CPA who once worked for a Big 8 accounting firm, I was surprised that Robert had made the learning of these two subjects both fun and exciting. The process was so well disguised that while we were diligently working to get out of the "Rat Race," we quickly forgot we were learning.

Soon a product test turned into a fun afternoon with my daughter, talking about things we had never discussed before. As an accountant, playing a game that required an Income Statement and Balance Sheet was easy. So I had the time to help my daughter and the other players at my table with concepts they did not understand. I was the first person—and the only person in the entire test group—to get out of the "Rat Race" that day. I was out within 50 minutes, although the game went on for nearly three hours.

At my table was a banker, a business owner and a computer programmer. What greatly disturbed me was how little these people knew about either accounting or investing, subjects so important in their lives. I wondered how they managed their own financial affairs in real life. I could understand why my 19-year-old daughter would not understand, but these were grown adults, at least twice her age.

After I was out of the "Rat Race," for the next two hours I watched my daughter and these educated, affluent adults roll the dice and move their markers. Although I was glad they were all learning so much, I was disturbed by how much the adults did not know about the basics of simple accounting and investing. They had difficulty grasping the relationship between their Income Statement and their Balance Sheet. As they bought and sold assets, they had trouble remembering that each transaction could impact their monthly cash flow. I thought, how many millions of people are out there in the real world struggling financially, only because they have never been taught these subjects?

Thank goodness they're having fun and are distracted by the desire to win the game, I said to myself. After Robert ended the contest, he allowed us fifteen minutes to discuss and critique *CASHFLOW* among ourselves.

The business owner at my table was not happy. He did not like the game. "I don't need to know this," he said out loud. "I hire accountants, bankers and attorneys to tell me about this stuff."

To which Robert replied, "Have you ever noticed that there are a lot of accountants who aren't rich? And bankers, and attorneys, and stockbrokers and real estate brokers. They know a lot, and for the most part are smart people, but most of them are not rich. Since our schools do not teach people what the rich know, we take advice from these people. But one day, you're driving down the highway, stuck in traffic, struggling to get to work, and you look over to your right and you see your accountant stuck in the same traffic jam. You look to your left and you see your banker. That should tell you something."

The computer programmer was also unimpressed by the game: "I can buy software to teach me this."

The banker, however, was moved. "I studied this in school—the accounting part, that is—but I never knew how to apply it to real life. Now I know. I need to get myself out of the 'Rat Race.' "

But it was my daughter's comments that most touched me. "I had fun learning," she said. "I learned a lot about how money really works and how to invest."

Then she added: "Now I know I can choose a profession for the work I want to perform and not because of job security, benefits or how much I get paid. If I learn what this game teaches, I'm free to do and study what my heart wants to study. . .rather than study something because businesses are looking for certain job skills. If I learn this, I won't have to worry about job security and Social Security the way most of my classmates already do."

I was not able to stay and talk with Robert after we had played the game, but we agreed to meet later to further discuss his project. I knew he wanted to use the game to help others become more financially savvy, and I was eager to hear more about his plans.

My husband and I set up a dinner meeting with Robert and his wife within the next week. Although it was our first social get-together, we felt as if we had known each other for years.

We found out we had a lot in common. We covered the gamut, from sports and plays to restaurants and socio-economic issues. We talked about the changing world. We spent a lot of time discussing how most Americans have little or nothing saved for retirement, as well as the almost bankrupt state of Social Security and Medicare. Would my children be required to pay for the retirement of 75 million baby boomers? We wondered if people realize how risky it is to depend on a pension plan.

Robert's primary concern was the growing gap between the haves and have nots, in America and around the world. A self-taught, self-made entrepreneur who traveled the world putting investments together, Robert was able to retire at the age of 47. He came out of retirement because he shares the same concern I have for my own children. He knows that the world has changed, but education has not changed with it. According to Robert, children spend years in an antiquated educational system, studying subjects they will never use, preparing for a world that no longer exists.

"Today, the most dangerous advice you can give a child is 'Go to school, get good grades and look for a safe secure job,' " he likes to say. "That is old advice, and it's bad advice. If you could see what is happening in Asia, Europe, South America, you would be as concerned as I am."

It's bad advice, he believes, "because if you want your child to have a financially secure future, they can't play by the old set of rules. It's just too risky."

I asked him what he meant by "old rules?" .

"People like me play by a different set of rules from what you play by," he said. "What happens when a corporation announces a downsizing?"

"People get laid off," I said. "Families are hurt. Unemployment goes up."

"Yes, but what happens to the company, in particular a public company on the stock exchange?"

"The price of the stock usually goes up when the downsizing is announced," I said. "The market likes it when a company reduces its labor costs, either through automation or just consolidating the labor force in general."

"That's right," he said. "And when stock prices go up, people like me, the shareholders, get richer. That is what I mean by a different set of rules. Employees lose; owners and investors win."

Robert was describing not only the difference between an employee and employer, but also the difference between controlling your own destiny and giving up that control to someone else.

"But it's hard for most people to understand why that happens," I said. "They just think it's not fair."

7

"That's why it is foolish to simply say to a child, 'Get a good education,' " he said. "It is foolish to assume that the education the school system provides will prepare your children for the world they will face upon graduation. Each child needs more education. Different education. And they need to know the rules. The different sets of rules."

"There are rules of money that the rich play by, and there are the rules that the other 95 percent of the population plays by," he said. "And the 95 percent learns those rules at home and in school. That is why it's risky today to simply say to a child, 'Study hard and look for a job.' A child today needs a more sophisticated education, and the current system is not delivering the goods. I don't care how many computers they put in the classroom or how much money schools spend. How can the education system teach a subject that it does not know?"

So how does a parent teach their children, what the school does not? How do you teach accounting to a child? Won't they get bored? And how do you teach investing when as a parent you yourself are risk averse? Instead of teaching my children to simply play it safe, I decided it was best to teach them to play it smart.

"So how would you teach a child about money and all the things we've talked about?" I asked Robert. "How can we make it easy for parents especially when they don't understand it themselves?"

"I wrote a book on the subject, " he said.

"Where is it?"

"In my computer. It's been there for years in random pieces. I add to it occasionally but I've never gotten around to put it all together. I began writing it after my other book became a best seller, but I never finished the new one. It's in pieces."

And in pieces it was. After reading the scattered sections, I decided the book had merit and needed to be shared, especially in these changing times. We agreed to co-author Robert's book.

I asked him how much financial information he thought a child needed. He said it would depend on the child. He knew at a young age that he wanted to be rich and was fortunate enough to have a father figure who was rich and willing to guide him. Education is the foundation of success, Robert said. Just as scholastic skills are vitally important, so are financial skills and communication skills.

What follows is the story of Robert's two dads, a rich one and a poor one, that expounds on the skills he's developed over a lifetime. The contrast between two dads provides an important perspective. The book is supported, edited and assembled by me. For any accountants who read this book, suspend your academic book knowledge and open your mind to the theories Robert presents. Although many of them challenge the very fundamentals of generally accepted accounting principles, they provide a valuable insight into the way true investors analyze their investment decisions.

When we as parents advise our children to "go to school, study hard and get a good job," we often do that out of cultural habit. It has always been the right thing to do. When I met Robert, his ideas initially startled me. Having been raised by two fathers, he had been taught to strive for two different goals. His educated dad advised him to work for a corporation. His rich dad advised him to own the corporation. Both life paths required education, but the subjects of study were completely different. His educated dad encouraged Robert to be a smart person. His rich dad encouraged Robert to know how to hire smart people.

Having two dads caused many problems. Robert's real dad was the superintendent of education for the state of Hawaii. By the time Robert was 16, the threat of "If you don't get good grades, you won't get a good job" had little effect. He already knew his career path was to own corporations, not to work for them. In fact, if it had not been for a wise and persistent high school guidance counselor, Robert might not have gone on to college. He admits that. He was eager to start building his assets, but finally agreed that the college education would also be a benefit to him.

Truthfully, the ideas in this book are probably too far fetched and radical for most parents today. Some parents are having a hard enough time simply keeping their children in school. But in light of our changing times, as parents we need to be open to new and bold ideas. To encourage children to be employees is to advise your children to pay more than their fair share of taxes over a lifetime, with little or no promise of a pension. And it is true that taxes are a person's greatest expense. In fact, most families work from January to mid-May for the government just to cover their taxes. New ideas are needed and this book provides them.

Robert claims that the rich teach their children differently. They teach their children at home, around the dinner table. These ideas may not be the ideas you choose to discuss with your children, but thank you for looking at them. And I advise you to keep searching. In my opinion, as a mom and a CPA, the concept of simply getting good grades and finding a good job is an old idea. We need to advise our children with a greater degree of sophistication. We need new ideas and different education. Maybe telling our children to strive to be good employees while also striving to own their own investment corporation is not such a bad idea.

It is my hope as a mother that this book helps other parents. It is Robert's hope to inform people that anyone can achieve prosperity if they so choose. If today you are a gardener or a janitor or even unemployed, you have the ability to educate yourself and teach those you love to take care of themselves financially. Remember that financial intelligence is the mental process via which we solve our financial problems.

Today we are facing global and technological changes as great or even greater than those ever faced before. No one has a crystal ball, but one thing is for certain: Changes lie ahead that are beyond our reality. Who knows what the future brings? But whatever happens, we have two fundamental choices: play it safe or play it smart by preparing, getting educated and awakening your own and your children's financial genius.

— Sharon Lechter

For a FREE TAPE
"What my Rich Dad Taught Me About Money"
and a COLOR BROCHURE about
CASHFLOW™ 101, the board game,
call 1-800-308-3585

CHAPTER ONE

Rich Dad, Poor Dad

As narrated by Robert Kiyosaki

I had two fathers, a rich one and a poor one. One was highly educated and intelligent; he had a Ph.D. and completed four years of undergraduate work in less than two years. He then went on to Stanford University, the University of Chicago, and Northwestern University to do his advanced studies, all on full financial scholarships. The other father never finished the eighth grade.

Both men were successful in their careers, working hard all their lives. Both earned substantial incomes. Yet one struggled financially all his life. The other would become one of the richest men in Hawaii. One died leaving tens of millions of dollars to his family, charities and his church. The other left bills to be paid.

Both men were strong, charismatic and influential. Both men offered me advice, but they did not advise the same things. Both men believed strongly in education but did not recommend the same course of study.

If I had had only one dad, I would have had to accept or reject his advice. Having two dads advising me offered me the choice of contrasting points of view; one of a rich man and one of a poor man.

Instead of simply accepting or rejecting one or the other, I found myself thinking more, comparing and then choosing for myself.

The problem was, the rich man was not rich yet and the poor man not yet poor. Both were just starting out on their careers, and both were struggling with money and families. But they had very different points of view about the subject of money.

For example, one dad would say, "The love of money is the root of all evil." The other, "The lack of money is the root of all evil."

As a young boy, having two strong fathers both influencing me was difficult. I wanted to be a good son and listen, but the two fathers did not say the same things. The contrast in their points of view, particularly where money was concerned, was so extreme that I grew curious and intrigued. I began to start thinking for long periods of time about what each was saying.

Much of my private time was spent reflecting, asking myself questions such as, "Why does he say that?" and then asking the same question of the other dad's statement. It would have been much easier to simply say, "Yeah, he's right. I agree with that." Or to simply reject the point of view by saying, "The old man doesn't know what he's talking about." Instead, having two dads whom I loved forced me to think and ultimately choose a way of thinking for myself. As a process, choosing for myself turned out to be much more valuable in the long run, rather than simply accepting or rejecting a single point of view.

One of the reasons the rich get richer, the poor get poorer, and the middle class struggles in debt is because the subject of money is taught at home, not in school. Most of us learn about money from our parents. So what can a poor parent tell their child about money? They simply say "Stay in school and study hard." The child may graduate with excellent grades but with a poor person's financial programming and mind-set. It was learned while the child was young.

Money is not taught in schools. Schools focus on scholastic and professional skills, but not on financial skills. This explains how smart bankers, doctors and accountants who earned excellent grades in school may still struggle financially all of their lives. Our staggering national debt is due in large part to highly educated politicians and government officials making financial decisions with little or no training on the subject of money.

I often look ahead to the new millennium and wonder what will happen when we have millions of people who will need financial and medical assistance. They will be dependent on their families or the government for financial support. What will happen when Medicare and Social Security run out of money? How will a nation survive if teaching children about money continues to be left to parents—most of whom will be, or already are, poor?

Because I had two influential fathers, I learned from both of them. I had to think about each dad's advice, and in doing so, I gained valuable

14

insight into the power and effect of one's thoughts on one's life. For example, one dad had a habit of saying, "I can't afford it." The other dad forbade those words to be used. He insisted I say, "How can I afford it?" One is a statement, and the other is a question. One lets you off the hook, and the other forces you to think. My soon-to-be-rich dad would explain that by automatically saying the words "I can't afford it," your brain stops working. By asking the question "How can I afford it?" your brain is put to work. He did not mean buy everything you wanted. He was fanatical about exercising your mind, the most powerful computer in the world. "My brain gets stronger every day because I exercise it. The stronger it gets, the more money I can make." He believed that automatically saying "I can't afford it" was a sign of mental laziness.

Although both dads worked hard, I noticed that one dad had a habit of putting his brain to sleep when it came to money matters, and the other had a habit of exercising his brain. The long-term result was that one dad grew stronger financially and the other grew weaker. It is not much different from a person who goes to the gym to exercise on a regular basis versus someone who sits on the couch watching television. Proper physical exercise increases your chances for health, and proper mental exercise increases your chances for wealth. Laziness decreases both health and wealth.

My two dads had opposing attitudes in thought. One dad thought that the rich should pay more in taxes to take care of those less fortunate. The other said, "Taxes punish those who produce and reward those who don't produce."

One dad recommended, "Study hard so you can find a good company to work for." The other recommended, "Study hard so you can find a good company to buy."

One dad said, "The reason I'm not rich is because I have you kids." The other said, "The reason I must be rich is because I have you kids."

One encouraged talking about money and business at the dinner table. The other forbade the subject of money to be discussed over a meal.

One said, "When it comes to money, play it safe, don't take risks." The other said, "Learn to manage risk."

One believed, "Our home is our largest investment and our greatest asset." The other believed, "My house is a liability, and if your house is your largest investment, you're in trouble."

Both dads paid their bills on time, yet one paid his bills first while the other paid his bills last.

One dad believed in a company or the government taking care of you and your needs. He was always concerned about pay raises, retirement plans, medical benefits, sick leave, vacation days and other perks. He was impressed with two of his uncles who joined the military and earned a retirement and entitlement package for life after twenty years of active service. He loved the idea of medical benefits and PX privileges the military provided its retirees. He also loved the tenure system available through the university. The idea of job protection for life and job benefits seemed more important, at times, than the job. He would often say, "I've worked hard for the government, and I'm entitled to these benefits."

The other believed in total financial self-reliance. He spoke out against the "entitlement" mentality and how it was creating weak and financially needy people. He was emphatic about being financially competent.

One dad struggled to save a few dollars. The other simply created investments.

One dad taught me how to write an impressive resume so I could find a good job. The other taught me how to write strong business and financial plans so I could create jobs.

Being a product of two strong dads allowed me the luxury of observing the effects different thoughts have on one's life. I noticed that people really do shape their life through their thoughts.

For example, my poor dad always said, "I'll never be rich." And that prophesy became reality. My rich dad, on the other hand, always referred to himself as rich. He would say things like, "I'm a rich man, and rich people don't do this." Even when he was flat broke after a major financial setback, he continued to refer to himself as a rich man. He would cover himself by saying, "There is a difference between being poor and being broke. Broke is temporary, and poor is eternal."

My poor dad would also say, "I'm not interested in money," or "Money doesn't matter." My rich dad always said, "Money is power."

The power of our thoughts may never be measured or appreciated, but it became obvious to me as a young boy to be aware of my thoughts and how I expressed myself. I noticed that my poor dad was poor not because of the amount of money he earned, which was significant, but because of his thoughts and actions. As a young boy, having two fathers, I became acutely aware of being careful which thoughts I chose to adopt as my own. Whom should I listen to—my rich dad or my poor dad?

Although both men had tremendous respect for education and learning, they disagreed in what they thought was important to learn. One wanted me to study hard, earn a degree and get a good job to work for money. He wanted me to study to become a professional, an attorney or an accountant or to go to business school for my MBA. The other encouraged me to study to be rich, to understand how money works and to learn how to have it work for me. "I don't work for money!" were words he would repeat over and over, "Money works for me!"

At the age of 9, I decided to listen to and learn from my rich dad about money. In doing so, I chose not to listen to my poor dad, even though he was the one with all the college degrees.

A Lesson From Robert Frost

Robert Frost is my favorite poet. Although I love many of his poems, my favorite is The Road Not Taken. I use its lesson almost daily:

The Road Not Taken

Two roads diverged in a yellow wood,
And sorry I could not travel both
And be one traveler, long I stood
And looked down one as far as I could
To where it bent in the undergrowth;

Then took the other, as just as fair,
And having perhaps the better claim,
Because it was grassy and wanted wear
Though as for that the passing there
Had worn them really about the same,

And both that morning equally lay
In leaves no step had trodden black.
Oh, I kept the first for another day!
Yet knowing how way leads onto way,
I doubted if I should ever come back.

I shall be telling this with a sigh
Somewhere ages and ages hence;
Two roads diverged in a wood, and I—
I took the one less traveled by,
And that has made all the difference.

Robert Frost [1916]

And that made all the difference.

Over the years, I have often reflected upon Robert Frost's poem. Choosing not to listen to my highly educated dad's advice and attitude about money was a painful decision, but it was a decision that shaped the rest of my life.

Once I made up my mind whom to listen to, my education about money began. My rich dad taught me over a period of 30 years, until I was age 39. He stopped once he realized that I knew and fully understood what he had been trying to drum into my often thick skull.

Money is one form of power. But what is more powerful is financial education. Money comes and goes, but if you have the education about how money works, you gain power over it and can begin building wealth. The reason positive thinking alone does not work is because most people went to school and never learned how money works, so they spend their lives working for money.

Because I was only 9 years old when I started, the lessons my rich dad taught me were simple. And when it was all said and done, there were only six main lessons, repeated over 30 years. This book is about those six lessons, put as simply as possible as my rich dad put forth those lessons to me. The lessons are not meant to be answers but guideposts. Guideposts that will assist you and your children to grow wealthier no matter what happens in a world of increasing change and uncertainty.

CHAPTER TWO
Lesson One:

The Rich Don't Work For Money

"*D*ad, Can You Tell Me How to Get Rich?"

My dad put down the evening paper. "Why do you want to get rich, son?"

"Because today Jimmy's mom drove up in their new Cadillac, and they were going to their beach house for the weekend. He took three of his friends, but Mike and I weren't invited. They told us we weren't invited because we were 'poor kids'."

"They did?" my dad asked incredulously.

"Yeah, they did." I replied in a hurt tone.

My dad silently shook his head, pushed his glasses up the bridge of his nose and went back to reading the paper. I stood waiting for an answer.

The year was 1956. I was 9 years old. By some twist of fate, I attended the same public school where the rich people sent their kids. We were primarily a sugar plantation town. The managers of the plantation and the other affluent people of the town, such as doctors, business owners, and bankers, sent their children to this school, grades 1 to 6. After grade 6, their children were generally sent off to private schools. Because my family lived on one side of the street, I went to this school. Had I lived on the other side of the street, I would have gone to a different school, with kids from families more like mine. After grade 6, these kids and I would go on to the public intermediate and high school. There was no private school for them or for me.

My dad finally put down the paper. I could tell he was thinking.

"Well, son," he began slowly. "If you want to be rich, you have to learn to make money."

"How do I make money?" I asked.

"Well, use your head, son," he said, smiling. Which really meant, "That's all I'm going to tell you," or "I don't know the answer, so don't embarrass me."

A Partnership Is Formed

The next morning, I told my best friend, Mike, what my dad had said. As best I could tell, Mike and I were the only poor kids in this school. Mike was like me in that he was in this school by a twist of fate. Someone had drawn a jog in the line for the school district, and we wound up in school with the rich kids. We weren't really poor, but we felt as if we were because all the other boys had new baseball gloves, new bicycles, new everything.

Mom and dad provided us with the basics, like food, shelter, clothes. But that was about it. My dad used to say, "If you want something, work for it." We wanted things, but there was not much work available for 9-year-old boys.

"So what do we do to make money?" Mike asked.

"I don't know," I said. "But do you want to be my partner?"

He agreed and so on that Saturday morning, Mike became my first business partner. We spent all morning coming up with ideas on how to make money. Occasionally we talked about all the "cool guys" at Jimmy's beach house having fun. It hurt a little, but that hurt was good, for it inspired us to keep thinking of a way to make money. Finally, that afternoon, a bolt of lightning came through our heads. It was an idea Mike had gotten from a science book he had read. Excitedly, we shook hands, and the partnership now had a business.

For the next several weeks, Mike and I ran around our neighborhood, knocking on doors and asking our neighbors if they would save their toothpaste tubes for us. With puzzled looks, most adults consented with a smile. Some asked us what we were doing. To which we replied, "We can't tell you. It's a business secret."

My mom grew distressed as the weeks wore on. We had selected a site next to her washing machine as the place we would stockpile our raw materials. In a brown cardboard box that one time held catsup bottles, our little pile of used toothpaste tubes began to grow.

Finally my mom put her foot down. The sight of her neighbors' messy, crumpled used toothpaste tubes had gotten to her. "What are you boys doing?" she asked. "And I don't want to hear again that it's a business secret. Do something with this mess or I'm going to throw it out."

Mike and I pleaded and begged, explaining that we would soon have enough and then we would begin production. We informed her that we were waiting on a couple of neighbors to finish using up their toothpaste so we could have their tubes. Mom granted us a one-week extension.

The date to begin production was moved up. The pressure was on. My first partnership was already being threatened with an eviction notice from our warehouse space by my own mom. It became Mike's job to tell the neighbors to quickly use up their toothpaste, saying their dentist wanted them to brush more often anyway. I began to put together the production line.

One day my dad drove up with a friend to see two 9-year-old boys in the driveway with a production line operating at full speed. There was fine white powder everywhere. On a long table were small milk cartons from school, and our family's hibachi grill was glowing with red hot coals at maximum heat.

Dad walked up cautiously, having to park the car at the base of the driveway, since the production line blocked the carport. As he and his friend got closer, they saw a steel pot sitting on top of the coals, with the toothpaste tubes being melted down. In those days, toothpaste did not come in plastic tubes. The tubes were made of lead. So once the paint was burned off, the tubes were dropped in the small steel pot, melted until they became liquid, and with my mom's pot holders we were pouring the lead through a small hole in the top of the milk cartons.

The milk cartons were filled with plaster-of-paris. The white powder everywhere was the plaster before we mixed it with water. In my haste, I had knocked the bag over, and the entire area look like it had been hit by a snowstorm. The milk cartons were the outer containers for plaster-of-paris molds.

My dad and his friend watched as we carefully poured the molten lead through a small hole in the top of the plaster-of-paris cube.

"Careful," my dad said.

I nodded without looking up.

Finally, once the pouring was through, I put the steel pot down and smiled at my dad.

"What are you boys doing?" he asked with a cautious smile.

"We're doing what you told me to do. We're going to be rich," I said.

"Yup," said Mike, grinning and nodding his head. "We're partners."

"And what is in those plaster molds?" dad asked.

"Watch," I said. "This should be a good batch."

With a small hammer, I tapped at the seal that divided the cube in half. Cautiously, I pulled up the top half of the plaster mold and a lead nickel fell out."

"Oh, my God!" my dad said. "You're casting nickels out of lead."

"That's right," Mike said. "We doing as you told us to do. We're making money."

My dad's friend turned and burst into laughter. My dad smiled and shook his head. Along with a fire and a box of spent toothpaste tubes, in front of him were two little boys covered with white dust and smiling from ear to ear.

He asked us to put everything down and sit with him on the front step of our house. With a smile, he gently explained what the word "counterfeiting" meant.

Our dreams were dashed. "You mean this is illegal?" asked Mike in a quivering voice.

"Let them go," my dad's friend said. "They might be developing a natural talent."

My dad glared at him.

"Yes, it is illegal," my dad said gently. "But you boys have shown great creativity and original thought. Keep going. I'm really proud of you!"

Disappointed, Mike and I sat in silence for about twenty minutes before we began cleaning up our mess. The business was over on opening day. Sweeping the powder up, I looked at Mike and said, "I guess Jimmy and his friends are right. We are poor."

My father was just leaving as I said that. "Boys," he said. "You're only poor if you give up. The most important thing is that you did something. Most people only talk and dream of getting rich. You've done something. I'm very proud of the two of you. I will say it again.

Keep going. Don't quit."

Mike and I stood there in silence. They were nice words, but we still did not know what to do.

"So how come you're not rich, dad?" I asked.

"Because I chose to be a schoolteacher. Schoolteachers really don't think about being rich. We just like to teach. I wish I could help you, but I really don't know how to make money."

Mike and I turned and continued our clean up.

"I know," said my dad. "If you boys want to learn how to be rich, don't ask me. Talk to your dad, Mike."

"My dad?" asked Mike with a scrunched up face.

"Yeah, your dad," repeated my dad with a smile. "Your dad and I have the same banker, and he raves about your father. He's told me several times that your father is brilliant when it comes to making money."

"My dad?" Mike asked again in disbelief. "Then how come we don't have a nice car and a nice house like the rich kids at school?"

"A nice car and a nice house does not necessarily mean you're rich or you know how to make money," my dad replied. "Jimmy's dad works for the sugar plantation. He's not much different from me. He works for a company, and I work for the government. The company buys the car for him. The sugar company is in financial trouble, and Jimmy's dad may soon have nothing. Your dad is different Mike. He seems to be building an empire, and I suspect in a few years he will be a very rich man."

With that, Mike and I got excited again. With new vigor, we began cleaning up the mess caused by our now defunct first business. As we were cleaning, we made plans on how and when to talk to Mike's dad. The problem was that Mike's dad worked long hours and often did not come home until late. His father owned warehouses, a construction company, a chain of stores, and three restaurants. It was the restaurants that kept him out late.

Mike caught the bus home after we had finished cleaning up. He was going to talk to his dad when he got home that night and ask him if he would teach us how to become rich. Mike promised to call as soon as he had talked to his dad, even if it was late.

The phone rang at 8:30 p.m.

"OK," I said. "Next Saturday." And put the phone down. Mike's dad had agreed to meet with Mike and me.

At 7:30 Saturday morning, I caught the bus to the poor side of town.

The Lessons Begin:

> *"I'll pay you 10 cents an hour."*
> *Even by 1956 pay standards, 10 cents an hour was low.*

Michael and I met with his dad that morning at 8 o'clock. He was already busy and had been at work for more than an hour. His construction supervisor was just leaving in his pickup truck as I walked up to his simple, small and tidy home. Mike met me at the door.

"Dad's on the phone, and he said to wait on the back porch," Mike said as he opened the door.

The old wooden floor creaked as I stepped across the threshold of this aging house. There was a cheap mat just inside the door. The mat was there to hide the years of wear from countless footsteps that the floor had supported. Although clean, it needed to be replaced.

I felt claustrophobic as I entered the narrow living room, which was filled with old musty overstuffed furniture that today would be collector's items. Sitting on the couch were two women, a little older than my mom. Across from the women sat a man in workman's clothes. He wore khaki slacks and a khaki shirt, neatly pressed but without starch, and polished work books. He was about 10 years older than my dad; I'd say about 45 years old. They smiled as Mike and I walked past them, heading for the kitchen, which lead to the porch that overlooked the back yard. I smiled back shyly.

"Who are those people?" I asked.

"Oh, they work for my dad. The older man runs his warehouses, and the women are the managers of the restaurants. And you saw the construction supervisor, who is working on a road project about 50 miles from here. His other supervisor, who is building a track of houses, had already left before you got here."

"Does this go on all the time?" I asked.

"Not always, but quite often," said Mike, smiling as he pulled up a chair to sit down next to me.

"I asked him if he would teach us to make money," Mike said.

"Oh, and what did he say to that?" I asked with cautious curiosity.

"Well, he had a funny look on his face at first, and then he said he would make us an offer."

"Oh," I said, rocking my chair back against the wall; I sat there perched on two rear legs of the chair.

Mike did the same thing.

"Do you know what the offer is?" I asked.

"No, but we'll soon find out."

Suddenly, Mike's dad burst through the rickety screen door and onto the porch. Mike and I jumped to our feet, not out of respect but because we were startled.

"Ready boys?" Mike's dad asked as he pulled up a chair to sit down with us.

We nodded our heads as we pulled our chairs away from the wall to sit in front of him.

He was a big man, about 6 feet tall and 200 pounds. My dad was taller, about the same weight, and five years older than Mike's dad. They sort of looked alike, though not of the same ethnic makeup. Maybe their energy was similar.

"Mike says you want to learn to make money? Is that correct, Robert?"

I nodded my head quickly, but with a little intimidation. He had a lot of power behind his words and smile.

"OK, here's my offer. I'll teach you, but I won't do it classroom-style. You work for me, I'll teach you. You don't work for me, I won't teach you. I can teach you faster if you work, and I'm wasting my time if you just want to sit and listen, like you do in school. That's my offer. Take it or leave it."

"Ah... may I ask a question first?" I asked.

"No. Take it or leave it. I've got too much work to do to waste my time. If you can't make up you mind decisively, then you'll never learn to make money anyway. Opportunities come and go. Being able to know when to make quick decisions is an important skill. You have an opportunity that you asked for. School is beginning or it's over in ten seconds," Mike's dad said with a teasing smile.

"Take it," I said.

"Take it," said Mike.

"Good," said Mike's dad. "Mrs. Martin will be by in ten minutes. After I'm through with her, you ride with her to my superette and you can begin working. I'll pay you 10 cents an hour and you will work for three hours every Saturday."

"But I have a softball game today," I said.

Mike's dad lowered his voice to a stern tone. "Take it or leave it," he said.

"I'll take it," I replied, choosing to work and learn instead of playing softball.

30 Cents Later

By 9 a.m. on a beautiful Saturday morning, Mike and I were working for Mrs. Martin. She was a kind and patient woman. She always said that Mike and I reminded her of her two sons who were grown and gone. Although kind, she believed in hard work and she kept us working. She was a task master. We spent three hours taking canned goods off the shelves and, with a feather duster, brushing each can to get the dust off, and then re-stacking them neatly. It was excruciatingly boring work.

Mike's dad, whom I call my rich dad, owned nine of these little superettes with large parking lots. They were the early version of the 7-11 convenience stores. Little neighborhood grocery stores where people bought items such as milk, bread, butter and cigarettes. The problem was, this was Hawaii before air conditioning, and the stores could not close its doors because of the heat. On two sides of the store, the doors had to be wide open to the road and parking lot. Every time a car drove by or pulled into the parking lot, dust would swirl and settle in the store.

Hence, we had a job for as long as there was no air conditioning.

For three weeks, Mike and I reported to Mrs. Martin and worked our three hours. By noon, our work was over, and she dropped three little dimes in each of our hands. Now, even at the age of 9 in the mid-1950s, 30 cents was not too exciting. Comic books cost 10 cents back then, so I usually spent my money on comic books and went home.

By Wednesday of the fourth week, I was ready to quit. I had agreed to work only because I wanted to learn to make money from Mike's dad, and now I was a slave for 10 cents an hour. On top of that, I had not seen Mike's dad since that first Saturday.

"I'm quitting," I told Mike at lunchtime. The school lunch was miserable. School was boring, and now I did not even have my Saturdays to look forward to. But it was the 30 cents that really got to me.

This time Mike smiled.

30

"What are you laughing at?" I asked with anger and frustration.

"Dad said this would happen. He said to meet with him when you were ready to quit."

"What?" I said indignantly. "He's been waiting for me to get fed up?"

"Sort of," Mike said. "Dad's kind of different. He teaches differently from your dad. Your mom and dad lecture a lot. My dad is quiet and a man of few words. You just wait till this Saturday. I'll tell him you're ready."

"You mean I've been set up?"

"No, not really, but maybe. Dad will explain on Saturday."

Waiting in Line on Saturday

I was ready to face him and I was prepared. Even my real dad was angry with him. My real dad, the one I call the poor one, thought that my rich dad was violating child labor laws and should be investigated.

My educated poor dad told me to demand what I deserve. At least 25 cents an hour. My poor dad told me that if I did not get a raise, I was to quit immediately.

"You don't need that damned job anyway," said my poor dad with indignity.

At 8 o'clock Saturday morning, I was going through the same rickety door of Mike's house.

"Take a seat and wait in line," Mike's dad said as I entered. He turned and disappeared into his little office next to a bedroom.

I looked around the room and did not see Mike anywhere. Feeling awkward, I cautiously sat down next to the same two women who where there four weeks earlier. They smiled and slid across the couch to make room for me.

Forty-five minutes went by, and I was steaming. The two women had met with him and left thirty minutes earlier. An older gentleman was in there for twenty minutes and was also gone.

The house was empty, and I sat out in his musty dark living room on a beautiful sunny Hawaiian day, waiting to talk to a cheapskate who exploited children. I could hear him rustling around the office, talking on the phone, and ignoring me. I was now ready to walk out, but for some reason I stayed.

Finally, fifteen minutes later, at exactly 9 o'clock, rich dad walked out of his office, said nothing, and signaled with his hand for me to enter his dingy office.

"I understand you want a raise or you're going to quit," rich dad said as he swiveled in his office chair.

"Well, you're not keeping your end of the bargain," I blurted out nearly in tears. It was really frightening for a 9-year-old boy to confront a grownup.

"You said that you would teach me if I worked for you. Well, I've worked for you. I've worked hard. I've given up my baseball games to work for you. And you don't keep your word. You haven't taught me anything. You are a crook like everyone in town thinks you are. You're greedy. You want all the money and don't take care of your employees. You make me wait and don't show me any respect. I'm only a little boy, and I deserve to be treated better."

Rich dad rocked back in his swivel chair, hands up to his chin, somewhat staring at me. It was like he was studying me.

"Not bad," he said. "In less than a month, you sound like most of my employees."

"What?" I asked. Not understanding what he was saying, I continued with my grievance. "I thought you were going to keep your end of the bargain and teach me. Instead you want to torture me? That's cruel. That's really cruel."

"I am teaching you," rich dad said quietly.

"What have you taught me? Nothing!" I said angrily. "You haven't even talked to me once since I agreed to work for peanuts. Ten cents an hour. Hah! I should notify the government about you.

We have child labor laws, you know. My dad works for the government, you know."

"Wow!" said rich dad. "Now you sound just like most of the people who used to work for me. People I've either fired or they've quit."

"So what do you have to say?" I demanded, feeling pretty brave for a little kid. "You lied to me. I've worked for you, and you have not kept your word. You haven't taught me anything."

"How do you know that I've not taught you anything?" asked rich dad calmly.

"Well, you've never talked to me. I've worked for three weeks, and you have not taught me anything," I said with a pout.

"Does teaching mean talking or a lecture?" rich dad asked.

"Well, yes," I replied.

"That's how they teach you in school," he said smiling. "But that is not how life teaches you, and I would say that life is the best teacher of all. Most of the time, life does not talk to you. It just sort of pushes you around. Each push is life saying, 'Wake up. There's something I want you to learn.' "

"What is this man talking about?" I asked myself silently. "Life pushing me around was life talking to me?" Now I knew I had to quit my job. I was talking to someone who needed to be locked up.

"If you learn life's lessons, you will do well. If not, life will just continue to push you around. People do two things. Some just let life push them around. Others get angry and push back. But they push back against their boss, or their job, or their husband or wife. They do not know it's life that's pushing."

I had no idea what he was talking about.

"Life pushes all of us around. Some give up. Others fight. A few learn the lesson and move on. They welcome life pushing them around. To these few people, it means they need and want to learn something. They learn and move on. Most quit, and a few like you fight."

Rich dad stood and shut the creaky old wooden window that needed repair. "If you learn this lesson, you will grow into a wise, wealthy and happy young man. If you don't, you will spend your life blaming a job, low pay or your boss for your problems. You'll live life hoping for that big break that will solve all your money problems."

Rich dad looked over at me to see if I was still listening. His eyes met mine. We stared at each other, streams of communication going between us through our eyes. Finally, I pulled away once I had absorbed his last message. I knew he was right. I was blaming him, and I did ask to learn. I was fighting.

Rich dad continued. "Or if you're the kind of person who has no guts, you just give up every time life pushes you. If you're that kind of person, you'll live all your life playing it safe, doing the right things, saving yourself for some event that never happens. Then, you die a boring old man. You'll have lots of friends who really like you because you were such a nice hard-working guy. You spent a life playing it safe, doing the right things. But the truth is, you let life push you into submission. Deep down you were terrified of taking risks. You really wanted to win, but the fear of losing was greater than the excitement of winning. Deep inside, you and only you will know you didn't go for it.

You chose to play it safe."

Our eyes met again. For ten seconds, we looked at each other, only pulling away once the message was received.

"You've been pushing me around?" I asked.

"Some people might say that," smiled rich dad. "I would say that I just gave you a taste of life."

"What taste of life?" I asked, still angry, but now curious. Even ready to learn.

"You boys are the first people that have ever asked me to teach them how to make money. I have more than 150 employees, and not one of them has asked me what I know about money. They ask me for a job and a paycheck, but never to teach them about money. So most will spend the best years of their lives working for money, not really understanding what it is they are working for."

I sat there listening intently.

"So when Mike told me about you wanting to learn how to make money, I decided to design a course that was close to real life. I could talk until I was blue in the face, but you wouldn't hear a thing. So I decided to let life push you around a bit so you could hear me. That's why I only paid you 10 cents."

"So what is the lesson I learned from working for only 10 cents an hour?" I asked. "That you're cheap and exploit your workers?"

Rich dad rocked back and laughed heartily. Finally, after his laughing stopped, he said, "You'd best change your point of view. Stop blaming me, thinking I'm the problem. If you think I'm the problem, then you have to change me. If you realize that you're the problem, then you can change yourself, learn something and grow wiser. Most people want everyone else in the world to change but themselves. Let me tell you, it's easier to change yourself than everyone else."

"I don't understand," I said.

"Don't blame me for your problems," rich dad said, growing impatient.

"But you only pay me 10 cents."

"So what are you learning?" rich dad asked, smiling.

"That you're cheap," I said with a sly grin.

"See, you think I'm the problem," said rich dad.

"But you are."

"Well, keep that attitude and you learn nothing. Keep the attitude that I'm the problem and what choices do you have?"

"Well, if you don't pay me more or show me more respect and teach me, I'll quit."

"Well put," rich dad said. "And that's exactly what most people do. They quit and go looking for another job, better opportunity, and higher pay, actually thinking that a new job or more pay will solve the problem. In most cases, it won't."

"So what will solve the problem?" I asked. "Just take this measly 10 cents an hour and smile?"

Rich dad smiled. "That's what the other people do. Just accept a paycheck knowing that they and their family will struggle financially. But that's all they do, waiting for a raise thinking that more money will solve the problem. Most just accept it, and some take a second job working harder, but again accepting a small paycheck."

I sat staring at the floor, beginning to understand the lesson rich dad was presenting. I could sense it was a taste of life. Finally, I looked up and repeated the question. "So what will solve the problem?"

"This," he said tapping me gently on the head. "This stuff between your ears."

It was at that moment that rich dad shared the pivotal point of view that separated him from his employees and my poor dad—and led him to eventually become one of the richest men in Hawaii while my highly educated, but poor, dad struggled financially all his life. It was a singular point of view that made all the difference over a lifetime.

Rich dad said over and over, this point of view, which I call Lesson No.1.

"The poor and the middle class work for money. The rich have money work for them."

On that bright Saturday morning, I was learning a completely different point of view from what I had been taught by my poor dad. At the age of 9, I grew aware that both dads wanted me to learn. Both dads encouraged me to study... but not the same things.

My highly educated dad recommended that I do what he did. "Son, I want you to study hard, get good grades, so you can find a safe, secure job with a big company. And make sure it has excellent benefits." My rich dad wanted me to learn how money works so I could make it work for me. These lessons I would learn through life with his guidance, not because of a classroom.

My rich dad continued my first lesson, "I'm glad you got angry about working for 10 cents an hour. If you had not gotten angry and had gladly accepted it, I would have to tell you that I could not teach you. You see, true learning takes energy, passion, a burning desire. Anger is a big part of that formula, for passion is anger and love combined. When it comes to money, most people want to play it safe and feel secure. So passion does not direct them. Fear does."

"So is that why they'll take a job with low pay?" I asked.

"Yes," said rich dad. "Some people say I exploit people because I don't pay as much as the sugar plantation or the government. I say the people exploit themselves. It's their fear, not mine."

"But don't you feel you should pay them more?" I asked.

"I don't have to. And besides, more money will not solve the problem. Just look at your dad. He makes a lot of money, and he still can't pay his bills. Most people, given more money, only get into more debt."

"So that's why the 10 cents an hour," I said, smiling. "It's a part of the lesson."

"That's right," smiled rich dad. "You see, your dad went to school and got an excellent education, so he could get a high-paying job. Which he did. But he still has money problems because he never learned anything about money at school. On top of that, he believes in working for money."

"And you don't?" I asked.

"No, not really," said rich dad. "If you want to learn to work for money, then stay in school. That is a great place to learn to do that. But if you want to learn how to have money work for you, then I will teach you that. But only if you want to learn."

"Wouldn't everyone want to learn that?" I asked.

"No," said rich dad. "Simply because it's easier to learn to work for money, especially if fear is your primary emotion when the subject of money is discussed."

"I don't understand," I said with a frown.

"Don't worry about that for now. Just know that it's fear that keeps most people working at a job. The fear of not paying their bills. The fear of being fired. The fear of not having enough money. The fear of starting over. That's the price of studying to learn a profession or trade, and then working for money. Most people become a slave to money… and then get angry at their boss."

"Learning to have money work for you is a completely different course of study?" I asked.

"Absolutely," rich dad answered, "absolutely."

We sat in silence on that beautiful Hawaiian Saturday morning. My friends would have just been starting their Little League baseball game. But for some reason, I was now thankful I had decided to work for 10 cents an hour. I sensed that I was about to learn something my friends would not learn in school.

"Ready to learn?" asked rich dad.

"Absolutely," I said with a grin.

"I have kept my promise. I've been teaching you from afar," my rich dad said. "At 9 years old, you've gotten a taste of what it feels like to work for money. Just multiply your last month by fifty years and you will have an idea of what most people spend their life doing."

"I don't understand," I said.

"How did you feel waiting in line to see me? Once to get hired and once to ask for more money?"

"Terrible," I said.

"If you choose to work for money, that is what life is like for many people," said rich dad.

"And how did you feel when Mrs. Martin dropped three dimes in your hand for three hours' work?"

"I felt like it wasn't enough. It seemed like nothing. I was disappointed," I said.

"And that is how most employees feel when they look at their paychecks. Especially after all the tax and other deductions are taken out. At least you got 100 percent."

"You mean most workers don't get paid everything?" I asked with amazement.

"Heavens no!" said rich dad. "The government always takes its share first."

"How do they do that?" I asked.

"Taxes," said rich dad. "You're taxed when you earn. You're taxed when you spend. You're taxed when you save. You're taxed when you die."

"Why do people let the government do that to them?"

"The rich don't," said rich dad with a smile. "The poor and the middle class do. I'll bet you that I earn more than your dad, yet he pays more in taxes."

"How can that be?" I asked. As a 9-year-old boy, that made no sense to me. "Why would someone let the government do that to them?"

Rich dad sat there in silence. I guess he wanted me to listen instead of jabber away at the mouth.

Finally, I calmed down. I did not like what I had heard. I knew my dad complained constantly about paying so much in taxes, but really did nothing about it. Was that life pushing him around?

Rich dad rocked slowly and silently in his chair, just looking at me.

"Ready to learn?" he asked.

I nodded my head slowly.

"As I said, there is a lot to learn. Learning how to have money work for you is a lifetime study. Most people go to college for four years, and their education ends. I already know that my study of money will continue over my lifetime, simply because the more I find out, the more I find out I need to know. Most people never study the subject. They go to work, get their paycheck, balance their checkbooks, and that's it. On top of that, they wonder why they have money problems. Then, they think that more money will solve the problem. Few realize that it's their lack of financial education that is the problem."

"So my dad has tax problems because he doesn't understand money?" I asked, confused.

"Look," said rich dad. "Taxes are just one small section on learning how to have money work for you. Today, I just wanted to find out if you still have the passion to learn about money. Most people don't. They want to go to school, learn a profession, have fun at their work, and earn lots of money. One day they wake up with big money problems, and then they can't stop working. That's the price of only knowing how to work for money instead of studying how to have money work for you. So do you still have the passion to learn?" asked rich dad.

I nodded my head.

"Good," said rich dad. "Now get back to work. This time, I will pay you nothing."

"What?" I asked in amazement.

"You heard me. Nothing. You will work the same three hours every

Saturday, but this time you will not be paid 10 cents per hour. You said you wanted to learn to not work for money, so I'm not going to pay you anything."

I couldn't believe what I was hearing.

"I've already had this conversation with Mike. He's already working, dusting and stacking canned goods for free. You'd better hurry and get back there."

"That's not fair," I shouted. "You've got to pay something."

"You said you wanted to learn. If you don't learn this now, you'll grow up to be like the two women and the older man sitting in my living room, working for money and hoping I don't fire them. Or like your dad, earning lots of money only to be in debt up to his eyeballs, hoping more money will solve the problem. If that's what you want, I'll go back to our original deal of 10 cents an hour. Or you can do what most people grow up to do. Complain that there is not enough pay, quit and go looking for another job."

"But what do I do?" I asked.

Rich dad tapped me on the head. "Use this," he said. "If you use it well, you will soon thank me for giving you an opportunity, and you will grow into a rich man."

I stood there still not believing what a raw deal I had been handed. Here I came to ask for a raise, and now I was being told to keep working for nothing.

Rich dad tapped me on the head again and said, "Use this. Now get out of here and get back to work."

LESSON #1:   The Rich Don't Work For Money

I didn't tell my poor dad I wasn't being paid. He would not have understood, and I did not want to try to explain something that I did not yet understand myself.

For three more weeks, Mike and I worked for three hours, every Saturday, for nothing. The work didn't bother me, and the routine got easier. It was the missed baseball games and not being able to afford to buy a few comic books that got to me.

Rich dad stopped by at noon on the third week. We heard his truck pull up in the parking lot and sputter when the engine was turned off. He entered the store and greeted Mrs. Martin with a hug. After finding out how things were going in the store, he reached into the ice-cream freezer, pulled out two bars, paid for them, and signaled to Mike and me.

"Let's go for a walk boys."

We crossed the street, dodging a few cars, and walked across a large grassy field, where a few adults were playing softball. Sitting down at a remote picnic table, he handed Mike and me the ice-cream bars.

"How's it going boys?"

"OK," Mike said.

I nodded in agreement.

"Learn anything yet?" rich dad asked.

Mike and I looked at each other, shrugged our shoulders and shook our heads in unison.

Avoiding One of Life's Biggest Traps

"Well, you boys had better start thinking. You're staring at one of life's biggest lessons. If you learn the lesson, you'll enjoy a life of great freedom and security. If you don't learn the lesson, you'll wind up like Mrs. Martin and most of the people playing softball in this park. They work very hard, for little money, clinging to the illusion of job security, looking forward to a three-week vacation each year and a skimpy pension after forty-five years of work. If that excites you, I'll give you a raise to 25 cents an hour."

"But these are good hard-working people. Are you making fun of them?" I demanded.

A smile came over rich dad's face.

"Mrs. Martin is like a mother to me. I would never be that cruel. I may sound cruel because I'm doing my best to point something out to the two of you. I want to expand your point of view so you can see something. Something most people never have the benefit of seeing because their vision is too narrow. Most people never see the trap they are in."

Mike and I sat there uncertain of his message. He sounded cruel, yet we could sense he was desperately wanting us to know something.

With a smile, rich dad said, "Doesn't that 25 cents an hour sound good? Doesn't it make your heart beat a little faster."

I shook my head "no," but it really did. Twenty five cents an hour would be big bucks to me.

"OK, I'll pay you a dollar an hour," rich dad said, with a sly grin.

Now my heart was beginning to race. My brain was screaming,

"Take it. Take it." I could not believe what I was hearing. Still, I said nothing.

"OK, $2 an hour."

My little 9-year-old brain and heart nearly exploded. After all, it was 1956 and being paid $2 an hour would have made me the richest kid in the world. I couldn't imagine earning that kind of money. I wanted to say "yes." I wanted the deal. I could see a new bicycle, new baseball glove, and adoration of my friends when I flashed some cash. On top of that, Jimmy and his rich friends could never call me poor again. But somehow my mouth stayed silent.

Maybe my brain had overheated and blown a fuse. But deep down, I badly wanted that $2 an hour.

The ice cream had melted and was running down my hand. The ice-cream stick was empty, and under it was a sticky mess of vanilla and chocolate that ants were enjoying. Rich dad was looking at two boys staring back at him, eyes wide open and brains empty. He knew he was testing us, and he knew there was a part of our emotions that wanted to take the deal. He knew that each human being has a weak and needy part of their soul that can be bought. And he knew that each human being also had a part of their soul that was strong and filled with a resolve that could never be bought. It was only a question of which one was stronger. He had tested thousands of souls in his life. He tested souls every time he interviewed someone for a job.

"OK, $5 an hour."

Suddenly there was a silence from inside me. Something had changed. The offer was too big and had gotten ridiculous. Not too many grownups in 1956 made more than $5 an hour. The temptation disappeared, and a calm set in. Slowly I turned to my left to look at Mike. He looked back at me. The part of my soul that was weak and needy was silenced. The part of me that had no price took over. There was a calm and a certainty about money that entered my brain and my soul. I knew Mike had gotten to that point also.

"Good," rich dad said softly. "Most people have a price. And they have a price because of human emotions named fear and greed. First, the fear of being without money motivates us to work hard, and then once we get that paycheck, greed or desire starts us thinking about all the wonderful things money can buy. The pattern is then set."

"What pattern?" I asked.

"The pattern of get up, go to work, pay bills, get up, go to work, pay bills... Their lives are then run forever by two emotions, fear and greed. Offer them more money, and they continue the cycle by also increasing their spending. This is what I call the Rat Race."

"There is another way?" Mike asked.

"Yes," said rich dad slowly. "But only a few people find it."

"And what is that way?" Mike asked.

"That's what I hope you boys will find out as you work and study with me. That is why I took away all forms of pay."

"Any hints?" Mike asked. "We're kind of tired of working hard, especially for nothing."

"Well, the first step is telling the truth," said rich dad.

"We haven't been lying." I said.

"I did not say you were lying. I said to tell the truth," rich dad came back.

"The truth about what?" I asked.

"How you're feeling," rich dad said. "You don't have to say it to anyone else. Just yourself."

"You mean the people in this park, the people who work for you, Mrs. Martin, they don't do that?" I asked.

"I doubt it," said rich dad. "Instead, they feel the fear of not having money. Instead of confronting the fear, they react instead of think. They react emotionally instead of using their heads," rich dad said, tapping us on our heads. "Then, they get a few bucks in their hands, and again the emotion of joy and desire and greed take over, and again they react, instead of think."

"So their emotions do their thinking," Mike said.

"That's correct," said rich dad. "Instead of telling the truth about how they feel, they react to their feeling, fail to think. They feel the fear, they go to work, hoping that money will soothe the fear, but it doesn't. That old fear haunts them, and they go back to work, hoping again that money will calm their fears, and again it doesn't. Fear has them in this trap of working, earning money, working, earning money, hoping the fear will go away. But every day they get up, and that old fear wakes up with them. For millions of people, that old fear keeps them awake all night, causing a night of turmoil and worry. So they get up and go to work, hoping that a paycheck will kill that fear gnawing at their soul. Money is running their lives, and they refuse to tell the truth about that.

Money is in control of their emotions and hence their souls."

Rich dad sat quietly, letting his words sink in. Mike and I heard what he said, but really did not understand fully what he was talking about. I just knew that I often wondered why grownups hurried off to work. It did not seem like much fun, and they never looked that happy, but something kept them hurrying off to work.

Realizing we had absorbed as much as possible of what he was talking about, rich dad said, "I want you boys to avoid that trap. That is really what I want to teach you. Not just to be rich, because being rich does not solve the problem."

"It doesn't?" I asked, surprised.

"No, it doesn't. Let me finish the other emotion, which is desire. Some call it greed, but I prefer desire. It is perfectly normal to desire something better, prettier, more fun or exciting. So people also work for money because of desire. They desire money for the joy they think it can buy. But the joy that money brings is often short lived, and they soon need more money for more joy, more pleasure, more comfort, more security. So they keep working, thinking money will soothe their souls that is troubled by fear and desire. But money cannot do that."

"Even rich people?" Mike asked.

"Rich people included," said rich dad. "In fact, the reason many rich people are rich is not because of desire but because of fear. They actually think that money can eliminate that fear of not having money, of being poor, so they amass tons of it only to find out the fear gets worse. They now fear losing it. I have friends who keep working even though they have plenty. I know people who have millions who are more afraid now than when they were poor. They're terrified of losing all their money. The fears that drove them to get rich got worse. That weak and needy part of their soul is actually screaming louder. They don't want to lose the big houses, the cars, the high life that money has bought them. They worry about what their friends would say if they lost all their money. Many are emotionally desperate and neurotic, although they look rich and have more money."

"So is a poor man happier?" I asked.

"No, I don't think so," replied rich dad. "The avoidance of money is just as psychotic as being attached to money."

As if on cue, the town derelict went past our table, stopping by the large rubbish can and rummaging around in it. The three of us watched him with great interest, when before we probably would have just ignored him.

Rich dad pulled a dollar out of his wallet and gestured to the older man. Seeing the money, the derelict came over immediately, took the bill, thanked rich dad profusely and hurried off ecstatic with his good fortune.

"He's not much different from most of my employees," said rich dad. "I've met so many people who say, 'Oh, I'm not interested in money.' Yet they'll work at a job for eight hours a day. That's a denial of truth. If they weren't interested in money, then why are they working? That kind of thinking is probably more psychotic than a person who hoards money."

As I sat there listening to my rich dad, my mind was flashing back to the countless times my own dad said, "I'm not interested in money." He said those words often. He also covered himself by always saying, "I work because I love my job."

"So what do we do?" I asked. "Not work for money until all traces of fear and greed are gone?"

"No, that would be a waste of time," said rich dad. "Emotions are what make us human. Make us real. The word 'emotion' stands for energy in motion. Be truthful about your emotions, and use your mind and emotions in your favor, not against yourself."

"Whoa!" said Mike.

"Don't worry about what I just said. It will make more sense in years to come. Just be an observer, not a reactor, to your emotions. Most people do not know that it's their emotions that are doing the thinking. Your emotions are your emotions, but you have got to learn to do your own thinking."

"Can you give me an example?" I asked.

"Sure," replied rich dad. "When a person says, 'I need to find a job,' it's most likely an emotion doing the thinking. Fear of not having money generates that thought."

"But people do need money if they have bills to pay," I said.

"Sure they do," smiled rich dad. "All I'm saying is that it's fear that is all too often doing the thinking."

"I don't understand," said Mike.

"For example," said rich dad. "If the fear of not having enough money arises, instead of immediately running out to get a job so they can earn a few bucks to kill the fear, they instead might ask themselves this question. 'Will a job be the best solution to this fear over the long run?' In my opinion, the answer is 'no.' Especially when you look over a person's lifetime. A job is really a short-term solution to a long-term problem."

"But my dad is always saying, 'Stay in school, get good grades, so you can find a safe, secure job.' I spoke out, somewhat confused.

"Yes, I understand he says that," said rich dad, smiling. "Most people recommend that, and it's a good idea for most people. But people make that recommendation primarily out of fear."

"You mean my dad says that because he's afraid?"

"Yes," said rich dad. "He's terrified that you won't be able to earn money and won't fit into society. Don't get me wrong. He loves you and wants the best for you. And I think his fear is justified. An education and a job are important. But it won't handle the fear. You see, that same fear that makes him get up in the morning to earn a few bucks is the fear that is causing him to be so fanatical about you going to school."

"So what do you recommend?" I asked.

"I want to teach you to master the power of money. Not be afraid of it. And they don't teach that in school. If you don't learn it, you become a slave to money."

It was finally making sense. He did want us to widen our views. To see what Mrs. Martin could not see, his employees could not see, or my dad for that matter. He used examples that sounded cruel at the time, but I've never forgotten them. My vision widened that day, and I could begin to see the trap that lay ahead for most people.

"You see, we're all employees ultimately. We just work at different levels," said rich dad. "I just want you boys to have a chance to avoid the trap. The trap caused by those two emotions, fear and desire. Use them in your favor, not against you. That's what I want to teach you. I'm not interested in just teaching you to make a pile of money. That won't handle the fear or desire. If you don't first handle fear and desire, and you get rich, you'll only be a high-paid slave."

"So how do we avoid the trap?" I asked.

"The main cause of poverty or financial struggle is fear and ignorance, not the economy or the government or the rich. It's self-inflicted fear and ignorance that keeps people trapped. So you boys go to school and get your college degrees. I'll teach you how to stay out of the trap."

The pieces of the puzzle were appearing. My highly educated dad had a great education and a great career. But school never told him how to handle money or his fears. It became clear that I could learn different and important things from two fathers.

"So you've been talking about the fear of not having money. How does the desire of money affect our thinking?" Mike asked.

"How did you feel when I tempted you with a pay raise? Did you notice your desires rising?"

We nodded our heads.

"By not giving in to your emotions, you were able to delay your reactions and think. That is most important. We will always have emotions of fear and greed. From here on in, it is most important for you to use those emotions to your advantage and for the long term, and not simply let your emotions run you by controlling your thinking. Most people use fear and greed against themselves. That's the start of ignorance. Most people live their lives chasing paychecks, pay raises and job security because of the emotions of desire and fear, not really questioning where those emotion-driven thoughts are leading them. It's just like the picture of a donkey, dragging a cart, with its owner dangling a carrot just in front of the donkey's nose. The donkey's owner may be going where he wants to go, but the donkey is chasing an illusion. Tomorrow there will only be another carrot for the donkey."

"You mean the moment I began to picture a new baseball glove, candy and toys, that's like a carrot to a donkey?" Mike asked.

"Yeah. And as you get older, your toys get more expensive. A new car, a boat and a big house to impress your friends," said rich dad with a smile. "Fear pushes you out the door, and desire calls to you. Enticing you toward the rocks. That's the trap."

"So what's the answer," Mike asked.

"What intensifies fear and desire is ignorance. That is why rich people with lots of money often have more fear the richer they get. Money is the carrot, the illusion. If the donkey could see the whole picture, it might rethink its choice to chase the carrot."

Rich dad went on to explain that a human's life is a struggle between ignorance and illumination.

He explained that once a person stops searching for information and knowledge of one's self, ignorance sets in. That struggle is a moment-to-moment decision—to learn to open or close one's mind.

"Look, school is very, very important. You go to school to learn a skill or profession so as to be a contributing member of society. Every culture needs teachers, doctors, mechanics, artists, cooks, business people, police officers, firefighters, soldiers. Schools train them so our culture can thrive and flourish," said rich dad. "Unfortunately, for many people, school is the end, not the beginning."

There was a long silence. Rich dad was smiling. I did not comprehend everything he said that day. But as with most great teachers, whose words continue to teach for years, often long after they're gone, his words are still with me today.

"I've been a little cruel today," said rich dad. "Cruel for a reason. I want you to always remember this talk. I want you to always think of Mrs. Martin. I want you always to think of the donkey. Never forget, because your two emotions, fear and desire, can lead you into life's biggest trap, if you're not aware of them controlling your thinking. To spend your life living in fear, never exploring your dreams, is cruel. To work hard for money, thinking that money will buy you things that will make you happy is also cruel. To wake up in the middle of the night terrified about paying bills is a horrible way to live. To live a life dictated by the size of a paycheck is not really a life. Thinking that a job will make you feel secure is lying to yourself. That's cruel, and that's the trap I want you to avoid, if possible. I've seen how money runs people's lives. Don't let that happen to you. Please don't let money run your life."

A softball rolled under our table. Rich dad picked it up and threw it back.

"So what does ignorance have to do with greed and fear?" I asked.

"Because it is ignorance about money that causes so much greed and so much fear," said rich dad. "Let me give you some examples. A doctor, wanting more money to better provide for his family, raises his fees. By raising his fees, it makes health care more expensive for everyone. Now, it hurts the poor people the most, so poor people have worse health than those with money.

"Because the doctors raise their rates, the attorneys raise their rates. Because the attorneys' rates have gone up, schoolteachers want a raise, which raises our taxes, and on and on and on. Soon, there will be such a horrifying gap between the rich and the poor that chaos will break out and another great civilization will collapse. Great civilizations collapsed when the gap between the haves and havenots was too great. America is on the same course, proving once again that history repeats itself, because we do not learn from history. We only memorize historical dates and names, not the lesson.

"Aren't prices supposed to go up?" I asked.

"Not in an educated society with a well-run government. Prices should actually come down. Of course, that is often only true in theory. Prices go up because of greed and fear caused by ignorance. If schools taught people about money, there would be more money and lower prices, but schools focus only on teaching people to work for money, not how to harness money's power."

"But don't we have business schools?" Mike asked. "Aren't you encouraging me to go to business school for my master's degree?"

"Yes," said rich dad. "But all too often, business schools train employees who are sophisticated bean counters. Heaven forbid a bean counter takes over a business. All they do is look at the numbers, fire people and kill the business. I know because I hire bean counters. All they think about is cutting costs and raising prices, which cause more problems. Bean counting is important. I wish more people knew it, but it, too, is not the whole picture," added rich dad angrily.

"So is there an answer?" asked Mike.

"Yes," said rich dad. "Learn to use your emotions to think, not think with your emotions. When you boys mastered your emotions, first by agreeing to work for free, I knew there was hope. When you again resisted your emotions when I tempted you with more money, you were again learning to think in spite of being emotionally charged. That's the first step."

"Why is that step so important?" I asked.

"Well, that's up to you to find out. If you want to learn, I'll take you boys into the briar patch. That place where almost everyone else avoids. I'll take you to that place where most people are afraid to go. If you go with me, you'll let go of the idea of working for money and instead learn to have money work for you."

"And what will we get if we go with you. What if we agree to learn from you? What will we get?" I asked.

"The same thing Briar Rabbit got," said rich dad. "Freedom from the

Tar Baby."

"Is there a briar patch?" I asked.

"Yes," said rich dad. "The briar patch is our fear and our greed. Going into our fear and confronting our greed, our weaknesses, our neediness is the way out. And the way out is through the mind, by choosing our thoughts."

"Choosing our thoughts?" Mike asked, puzzled.

"Yes. Choosing what we think rather than reacting to our emotions. Instead of just getting up and going to work to solve your problems, just because the fear of not having the money to pay your bills is scaring you. Thinking would be taking the time to ask yourself a question. A question like, 'Is working harder at this the best solution to this problem?' Most people are so terrified at not telling themselves the truth—that fear is in control—that they cannot think, and instead run out the door. Tar baby is in control. That's what I mean by choosing your thoughts."

"And how do we do that?" Mike asked.

"That's what I will be teaching you. I'll be teaching you to have a choice of thoughts to consider, rather than knee-jerk reacting, like gulping down your morning coffee and running out the door.

"Remember what I said before: A job is only a short-term solution to a long-term problem. Most people have only one problem in mind, and it's short term. It's the bills at the end of the month, the Tar Baby. Money now runs their lives. Or should I say the fear and ignorance about money. So they do as their parents did, get up every day and go work for money. Not having the time to say, 'Is there another way?' Their emotions now control their thinking, not their heads."

"Can you tell the difference between emotions thinking and the head thinking?" Mike asked.

"Oh, yes. I hear it all the time," said rich dad. "I hear things like, 'Well, everyone has to work.' Or 'The rich are crooks.' Or 'I'll get another job. I deserve this raise. You can't push me around.' Or 'I like this job because it's secure.' Instead of, 'Is there something I'm missing here?' which breaks the emotional thought, and gives you time to think clearly."

I must admit, it was a great lesson to be getting. To know when someone was speaking out of emotions or out of clear thought. It was a lesson that served me well for life. Especially when I was the one speaking out of reaction and not from clear thought.

As we headed back to the store, rich dad explained that the rich really did "make money." They did not work for it. He went on to explain that when Mike and I were casting 5-cent pieces out of lead, thinking we were making money, we were very close to thinking the way the rich think. The problem was that it was illegal for us to do it. It was legal for the government and banks to do it, but not us. He explained that there are legal ways to make money and illegal ways.

Rich dad went on to explain that the rich know that money is an illusion, truly like the carrot for the donkey. It's only out of fear and greed that the illusion of money is held together by billions of people thinking that money is real. Money is really made up. It was only because of the illusion of confidence and the ignorance of the masses that the house of cards stood standing. "In fact," he said, "in many ways the donkey's carrot was more valuable than money."

He talked about the gold standard that America was on, and that each dollar bill was actually a silver certificate. What concerned him was the rumor that we would someday go off the gold standard and our dollars would no longer be silver certificates.

"When that happens, boys, all hell is going to break loose. The poor, the middle class and the ignorant will have their lives ruined simply because they will continue to believe that money is real and that the company they work for, or the government, will look after them."

We really did not understand what he was saying that day, but over the years it made more and more sense.

Seeing What Others Miss

As he climbed into his pickup truck, outside of his little convenience store, he said, "Keep working boys, but the sooner you forget about needing a paycheck, the easier your adult life will be. Keep using your brain, work for free, and soon your mind will show you ways of making money far beyond what I could ever pay you. You will see things that other people never see. Opportunities right in front of their noses. Most people never see these opportunities because they're looking for money and security, so that's all they get. The moment you see one opportunity, you will see them for the rest of your life. The moment you do that, I'll teach you something else. Learn this, and you'll avoid one of life's biggest traps. You'll never, ever, touch that Tar Baby."

Mike and I picked up our things from the store and waved goodbye to Mrs. Martin. We went back to the park, to the same picnic bench, and spent several more hours thinking and talking.

We spent the next week at school, thinking and talking. For two more weeks, we kept thinking, talking, and working for free.

At the end of the second Saturday, I was again saying goodbye to Mrs. Martin and looking at the comic-book stand with a longing gaze. The hard thing about not even getting 30 cents every Saturday was that I didn't have any money to buy comic books. Suddenly, as Mrs. Martin was saying goodbye to Mike and me, I saw something she was doing that I had never seen her do before. I mean, I had seen her do it, but I never took notice of it.

Mrs. Martin was cutting the front page of the comic book in half. She was keeping the top half of the comic book cover and throwing the rest of the comic book into a large brown cardboard box. When I asked her what she did with the comic books, she said, "I throw them away. I give the top half of the cover back to the comic-book distributor for credit when he brings in the new comics. He's coming in an hour."

Mike and I waited for an hour. Soon the distributor arrived and I asked him if we could have the comic books. To which he replied, "You can have them if you work for this store and do not resell them."

Our partnership was revived. Mike's mom had a spare room in the basement that no one used. We cleaned it out, and began piling hundreds of comic books in that room. Soon our comic-book library was open to the public. We hired Mike's younger sister, who loved to study, to be head librarian. She charged each child 10 cents admission to the library, which was open from 2:30 to 4:30 p.m. every day after school. The customers, the children of the neighborhood, could read as many comics as they could in two hours. It was a bargain for them since a comic costs 10 cents each, and they could read five or six in two hours.

Mike's sister would check the kids as they left, to make sure they weren't borrowing any comic books. She also kept the books, logging in how many kids showed up each day, who they were, and any comments they might have. Mike and I averaged $9.50 per week over a three-month period. We paid his sister $1 a week and allowed her to read the comics for free, which she rarely did since she was always studying.

Mike and I kept our agreement by working in the store every Saturday and collecting all the comic books from the different stores. We kept our agreement to the distributor by not selling any comic books. We burned them once they got too tattered. We tried opening a branch office, but we could never quite find someone as dedicated as Mike's sister we could trust.

At an early age, we found out how hard it was to find good staff.

Three months after the library first opened, a fight broke out in the room. Some bullies from another neighborhood pushed their way in and started it. Mike's dad suggested we shut down the business. So our comic-book business shut down, and we stopped working on Saturdays at the convenience store. Anyway, rich dad was excited because he had new things he wanted to teach us. He was happy because we had learned our first lesson so well. We had learned to have money work for us. By not getting paid for our work at the store, we were forced to use our imaginations to identify an opportunity to make money. By starting our own business, the comic-book library, we were in control of our own finances, not dependent on an employer. The best part was that our business generated money for us, even when we weren't physically there. Our money worked for us.

Instead of paying us money, rich dad had given us so much more.

WHY TEACH FINANCIAL LITERACY?

Why Teach Financial Literacy?

*I*n 1990, my best friend, Mike, took over his father's empire and is, in fact, doing a better job than his dad did. We see each other once or twice a year on the golf course. He and his wife are wealthier than you could imagine. Rich dad's empire is in great hands, and Mike is now grooming his son to take his place, as his dad had groomed us.

In 1994, I retired at the age of 47, and my wife, Kim, was 37. Retirement does not mean not working. To my wife and me, it means that barring unforeseen cataclysmic changes, we can work or not work, and our wealth grows automatically, staying way ahead of inflation. I guess it means freedom. The assets are large enough to grow by themselves. It's like planting a tree. You water it for years and then one day it doesn't need you anymore. It's roots have gone down deep enough. Then, the tree provides shade for your enjoyment.

Mike chose to run the empire and I chose to retire.

Whenever I speak to groups of people, they often ask what I would recommend or what could they do? "How do they get started?" "Is there a good book I would recommend?" "What should they do to prepare their children?" "What is the secret to success?" "How do I make millions?" I am always reminded of this article I was once given. It goes as follows.

THE RICHEST BUSINESSMEN

In 1923 a group of our greatest leaders and richest businessmen held a meeting at the Edgewater Beach hotel in Chicago. Among them were Charles Schwab, head of the largest independent steel company; Samuel Insull, president of the world's largest utility; Howard Hopson, head of the largest gas company; Ivar Kreuger president of the International Match Co., one of the world's largest companies at that time; Leon Frazier, president of the Bank of International Settlements; Richard Whitney, president of the New York Stock Exchange; Arthur Cotton and Jesse Livermore, two of the biggest stock speculators; and Albert Fall, a member of President Harding's cabinet. Twenty five years later nine of them (those listed above) ended as follows. Schwab died penniless after living for five years on borrowed money. Insull died broke living in a foreign land. Kreuger and Cotton also died broke. Hopson went insane. Whitney and Albert Fall were just released from prison. Fraser and Livermore committed suicide.

I doubt if anyone can say what really happened to these men. If you look at the date, 1923, it was just before the 1929 market crash and the Great Depression, which I suspect had a great impact on these men and their lives. The point is this: Today we live in times of greater and faster change than these men did. I suspect there will be many booms and busts in the next 25 years that will parallel the ups and downs these men faced. I am concerned that too many people are focused too much on money and not their greatest wealth, which is their education. If people are prepared to be flexible, keep an open mind and learn, they will grow richer and richer through the changes. If they think money will solve problems, I am afraid those people will have a rough ride. Intelligence solves problems and produces money. Money without financial intelligence is money soon gone.

Most people fail to realize that in life, it's not how much money you make, it's how much money you keep. We have all heard stories of lottery winners who are poor, then suddenly rich, then poor again. They win millions and are soon back to where they started. Or stories of professional athletes, who, at the age of 24, are earning millions of dollars a year, and are sleeping under a bridge by age 34. In the paper this morning, as I write this, there is a story of a young basketball player who a year ago had millions. Today, he claims his friends, attorney and accountant took his money, and now he works at a car wash for minimum wage.

He is only 29. He was fired from the car wash because he refused to take off his championship ring as he was wiping off the cars, so his story made the newspaper. He is appealing his termination, claiming hardship and discrimination and that the ring is all he has left. He claims that if you take that away, he'll crumble.

In 1997, I know so many people who are becoming instant millionaires. It's the Roaring '20s one more time. And while I am glad people have been getting richer and richer, I only caution that in the long run, it's not how much you make, it's how much you keep, and how many generations you keep it.

So when people ask, "Where do I get started?" or "Tell me how to get rich quick," they often are greatly disappointed with my answer. I simply say to them what my rich dad said back to me when I was a little kid. "If you want to be rich, you need to be financially literate."

That idea was drummed into my head every time we were together. As I said, my educated dad stressed the importance of reading books, while my rich dad stressed the need to master financial literacy.

If you are going to build the Empire State Building, the first thing you need to do is dig a deep hole and pour a strong foundation. If you are going to build a home in the suburbs, all you need to do is pour a 6-inch slab of concrete. Most people, in their drive to get rich, are trying to build an Empire State Building on a 6-inch slab.

Our school system, having been created in the Agrarian Age, still believes in homes with no foundation. Dirt floors are still the rage. So kids graduate from school with virtually no financial foundation. One day, sleepless and deep in debt in suburbia, living the American Dream, they decide that the answer to their financial problems is to find a way to get rich quick.

Construction on the skyscraper begins. It goes up quickly, and soon, instead of the Empire State Building, we have the Leaning Tower of Suburbia. The sleepless nights return.

As for Mike and me in our adult years, both of our choices were possible because we were taught to pour a strong financial foundation when we were just kids.

Now, accounting is possibly the most boring subject in the world. It also could be the most confusing. But if you want to be rich, long term, it could be the most important subject. The question is, how do you take a boring and confusing subject and teach it to kids? The answer is, make it simple. Teach it first in pictures.

My rich dad poured a strong financial foundation for Mike and me. Since we were just kids, he created a simple way to teach us. For years he only drew pictures and used words. Mike and I understood the simple drawings, the jargon, the movement of money, and then in later years, rich dad began adding numbers. Today, Mike has gone on to master much more complex and sophisticated accounting analysis because he has had to. He has a billion-dollar empire to run. I am not as sophisticated because my empire is smaller, yet we come from the same simple foundation. In the following pages, I offer to you the same simple line drawings Mike's dad created for us. Though simple, those drawings helped guide two little boys in building great sums of wealth on a solid and deep foundation.

Rule One. You must know the difference between an asset and a liability, and buy assets. If you want to be rich, this is all you need to know. It is Rule No. 1. It is the only rule. This may sound absurdly simple, but most people have no idea how profound this rule is. Most people struggle financially because they do not know the difference between an asset and a liability.

"Rich people acquire assets. The poor and middle class acquire liabilities, but they think they are assets"

When rich dad explained this to Mike and me, we thought he was kidding. Here we were, nearly teenagers and waiting for the secret to getting rich, and this was his answer. It was so simple that we had to stop for a long time to think about it.

"What is an asset?" asked Mike.

"Don't worry right now," said rich dad. "Just let the idea sink in. If you can comprehend the simplicity, your life will have a plan and be financially easy. It is simple; that is why the idea is missed."

"You mean all we need to know is what an asset is, acquire them and we'll be rich?" I asked.

Rich dad nodded his head. "It's that simple."

"If it's that simple, how come everyone is not rich?" I asked.

Rich dad smiled. "Because people do not know the difference

between an asset and a liability."

I remember asking, "How could adults be so silly. If it is that simple, if it is that important, why would everyone not want to find out?"

It took our rich dad only a few minutes to explain what assets and liabilities were.

As an adult, I have difficulty explaining it to other adults. Why? Because adults are smarter. In most cases, the simplicity of the idea escapes most adults because they have been educated differently. They have been educated by other educated professionals, such as bankers, accountants, real estate agents, financial planners, and so forth. The difficulty comes in asking adults to unlearn, or become children again. An intelligent adult often feels it is demeaning to pay attention to simplistic definitions.

Rich dad believed in the KISS principle—"Keep It Simple Stupid"—so he kept it simple for two young boys, and that made the financial foundation strong.

So what causes the confusion? Or how could something so simple be so screwed up? Why would someone buy an asset that was really a liability. The answer is found in basic education.

We focus on the word "literacy" and not "financial literacy." What defines something to be an asset, or something to be a liability are not words. In fact, if you really want to be confused, look up the words "asset" and "liability" in the dictionary. I know the definition may sound good to a trained accountant, but for the average person it makes no sense. But we adults are often too proud to admit that something does not make sense.

As young boys, rich dad said, "What defines an asset is not words but numbers. And if you cannot read the numbers, you cannot tell an asset from a hole in the ground."

"In accounting," rich dad would say, "it's not the numbers, but what the numbers are telling you. It's just like words. It's not the words, but the story the words are telling you.

Many people read, but do not understand much. It's called reading comprehension. And we all have different abilities when it comes to reading comprehension. For example, I recently bought a new VCR. It came with an instruction book that explained how to program the VCR. All I wanted to do was record my favorite TV show on Friday night. I nearly went crazy trying to read the manual. Nothing in my world is more complex than learning how to program my VCR. I could read the words, but I understood nothing. I get an "A" for recognizing the words. I get an "F" for comprehension. And so it is with financial statements for most people.

"If you want to be rich, you've got to read and understand numbers." If I heard that once, I heard it a thousand times from my rich dad. And I also heard, "The rich acquire assets and the poor and middle class acquire liabilities."

Here is how to tell the difference between an asset and a liability. Most accountants and financial professionals do not agree with the definitions, but these simple drawings were the start of strong financial foundations for two young boys.

To teach pre-teen boys, rich dad kept everything simple, using as many pictures as possible, as few words as possible, and no numbers for years.

"This is the Cash Flow pattern of an asset."

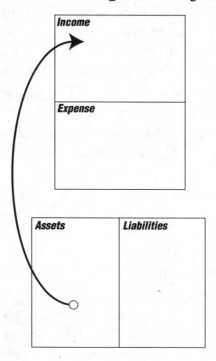

The above box is an Income Statement, often called a Profit and Loss Statement. It measures income and expenses. Money in and money out. The bottom diagram is the Balance Sheet. It is called that because it is supposed to balance assets against liabilities. Many financial novices do not know the relationship between the Income Statement and the Balance Sheet. That relationship is vital to understand.

The primary cause of financial struggle is simply not knowing the difference between an asset and a liability. The cause of the confusion is found in the definition of the two words. If you want a lesson in confusion, simply look up the words "asset" and "liability" in the dictionary.

Now it may make sense to trained accountants, but to the average person, it may as well be written in Mandarin. You read the words in the definition, but true comprehension is difficult.

So as I said earlier, my rich dad simply told two young boys that "assets put money in your pocket." Nice, simple and usable.

"This is Cash Flow pattern of a liability."

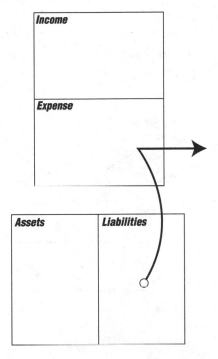

Now that assets and liabilities have been defined through pictures, it may be easier to understand my definitions in words.

An asset is something that puts money in my pocket.

A liability is something that takes money out of my pocket.

This is really all you need to know. If you want to be rich, simply spend your life buying assets. If you want to be poor or middle class, spend your life buying liabilities. It's not knowing the difference that causes most of the financial struggle in the real world.

Illiteracy, both in words and numbers, is the foundation of financial struggle. If people are having difficulties financially, there is something that they cannot read, either in numbers or words. Something is misunderstood. The rich are rich because they are more literate in different areas than people who struggle financially. So if you want to be rich and maintain your wealth, it's important to be financially literate, in words as well as numbers.

The arrows in the diagrams represent the flow of cash, or "cash flow." Numbers alone really mean little. Just as words alone mean little. It's the story that counts. In financial reporting, reading numbers is looking for the plot, the story. The story of where the cash is flowing. In 80 percent of most families, the financial story is a story of working hard in an effort to get ahead. Not because they don't make money. But because they spend their lives buying liabilities instead of assets.

For instance, this is the cash flow pattern of a poor person, or a young person still at home:

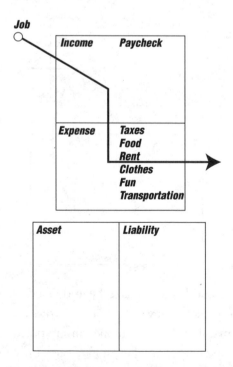

This is the cash flow pattern of a person in the middle class:

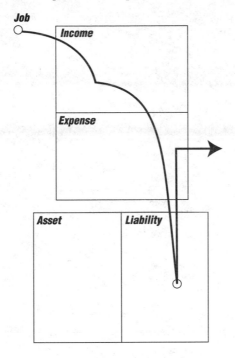

Job

Income	
	Paycheck

Expense	
	Taxes
	Mortgage
	Fixed Expense
	Food
	Clothing
	Fun

Asset	Liability
	Mortgage
	Consumer Loans
	Credit Cards

This is the cash flow pattern of a wealthy person:

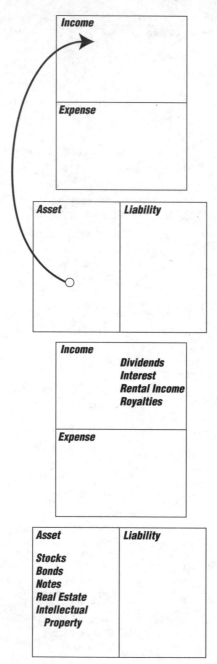

All of these diagrams were obviously oversimplified. Everyone has living expenses, the need for food, shelter and clothing.

The diagrams show the flow of cash through a poor, middle class or wealthy person's life. It is the cash flow that tells the story. It is the story of how a person handles their money, what they do after they get the money in their hand.

The reason I started with the story of the richest men in America is to illustrate the flaw in the thinking of so many people. The flaw is that money will solve all problems. That is why I cringe whenever I hear people ask me how to get rich quicker. Or where do they start? I often hear, "I'm in debt so I need to make more money."

But more money will often not solve the problem; in fact, it may actually accelerate the problem. Money often makes obvious our tragic human flaws. Money often puts a spotlight on what we do not know. That is why, all too often, a person who comes into a sudden windfall of cash—let's say an inheritance, a pay raise or lottery winnings—soon returns to the same financial mess, if not worse than the mess they were in before they received the money. Money only accentuates the cash-flow pattern running in your head. If your pattern is to spend everything you get, most likely an increase in cash will just result in an increase in spending. Thus, the saying, "A fool and his money is one big party."

I have said many times that we go to school to gain scholastic skills and professional skills, both important. We learn to make money with our professional skills. In the 1960s, when I was in high school, if someone did well in school academically, almost immediately people assumed this bright student would go on to be a medical doctor. Often no one asked the child if they wanted to be a doctor. It was assumed. It was the profession with the promise of the greatest financial reward.

Today, doctors are facing financial challenges I would not wish on my worst enemy: insurance companies taking control of the business, managed health care, government intervention, and malpractice suits, to name a few. Today, kids want to be basketball stars, golfers like Tiger Woods, computer nerds, movie stars, rock stars, beauty queens, or traders on Wall Street. Simply because that is where the fame, money and prestige is. That is the reason it is so hard to motivate kids in school today. They know that professional success is no longer solely linked to academic success, as it once was.

Because students leave school without financial skills, millions of educated people pursue their profession successfully, but later find themselves struggling financially. They work harder, but don't get ahead. What is missing from their education is not how to make money, but how to spend money—what to do after you make it. It's called financial aptitude—what you do with the money once you make it, how to keep people from taking it from you, how long you keep it, and how hard that money works for you. Most people cannot tell why they struggle financially because they don't understand cash flow. A person can be highly educated, professionally successful and financially illiterate. These people often work harder than they need to because they learned how to work hard, but not how to have their money work for them.

The story of how the quest for a Financial Dream turns into a financial nightmare

The moving-picture show of hard-working people has a set pattern. Recently married, the happy, highly educated young couple move in together, in one of their cramped rented apartments. Immediately, they realize that they are saving money because two can live as cheaply as one.

The problem is, the apartment is cramped. They decide to save money to buy their dream home so they can have kids. They now have two incomes, and they begin to focus on their careers.

Their incomes begin to increase.

As their incomes go up...

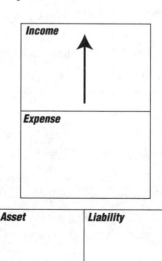

66

Their expenses go up as well.

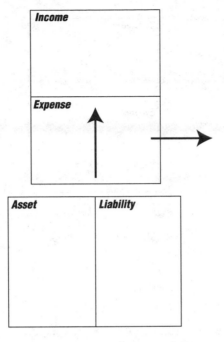

The No. 1 expense for most people is taxes. Many people think it's income tax, but for most Americans their highest tax is Social Security. As an employee, it appears as if the Social Security tax combined with the Medicare tax rate is roughly 7.5 percent, but it's really 15 percent since the employer must match the Social Security amount. In essence, it is money the employer cannot pay you. On top of that, you still have to pay income tax on the amount deducted from your wages for Social Security tax, income you never receive because it went directly to Social Security through withholding.

Then, their liabilities go up.

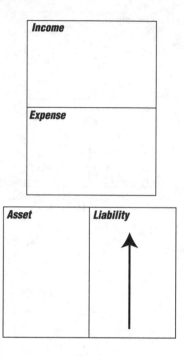

This is best demonstrated by going back to the young couple. As a result of their incomes going up, they decide to go out and buy the house of their dreams. Once in their house, they have a new tax, called property tax. Then, they buy a new car, new furniture and new appliances to match their new house. All of a sudden, they wake up and their liabilities column is full of mortgage debt and credit-card debt.

They're now trapped in the rat race. A child comes along. They work harder. The process repeats itself. More money and higher taxes, also called bracket creep. A credit card comes in the mail. They use it. It maxes out. A loan company calls and says their greatest "asset," their home, has appreciated in value. The company offers a "bill consolidation" loan, because their credit is so good, and tells them the intelligent thing to do is clear off the high-interest consumer debt by paying off their credit card. And besides, interest on their home is a tax deduction. They go for it, and pay off those high-interest credit cards. They breathe a sigh of relief. Their credit cards are paid off. They've now folded their consumer debt into their home mortgage. Their payments go down because they extend their debt over 30 years. It is the smart thing to do.

Their neighbor calls to invite them to go shopping—the Memorial Day sale is on. A chance to save some money. They say to themselves, "I won't buy anything. I'll just go look." But just in case they find something, they tuck that clean credit card inside their wallet.

I run into this young couple all the time. Their names change, but their financial dilemma is the same. They come to one of my talks to hear what I have to say. They ask me, "Can you tell us how to make more money?" Their spending habits have caused them to seek more income.

They don't even know that the trouble is really how they choose to spend the money they do have, and that is the real cause of their financial struggle. It is caused by financial illiteracy and not understanding the difference between an asset and a liability.

More money seldom solves someone's money problems. Intelligence solves problems. There is a saying a friend of mine says over and over to people in debt.

"If you find you have dug yourself into a hole... stop digging."

As a child, my dad often told us that the Japanese were aware of three powers: "The power of the sword, the jewel and the mirror."

The sword symbolizes the power of weapons. America has spent trillions of dollars on weapons and, because of this, is the supreme military presence in the world.

The jewel symbolizes the power of money. There is some degree of truth to the saying, "Remember the golden rule. He who has the gold makes the rules."

The mirror symbolizes the power of self-knowledge. This self-knowledge, according to Japanese legend, was the most treasured of the three.

The poor and middle class all too often allow the power of money to control them. By simply getting up and working harder, failing to ask themselves if what they do makes sense, they shoot themselves in the foot as they leave for work every morning. By not fully understanding money, the vast majority of people allow the awesome power of money to control them. The power of money is used against them.

If they used the power of the mirror, they would have asked themselves, "Does this make sense?" All too often, instead of trusting their inner wisdom, that genius inside of them, most people go along with the crowd. They do things because everybody else does it. They conform rather than question. Often, they mindlessly repeat what they have been told. Ideas such as "diversify" or "your home is an asset." "Your home is your biggest investment." "You get a tax break for going into greater debt." "Get a safe job." "Don't make mistakes." "Don't take risks."

It is said that the fear of public speaking is a fear greater than death for most people. According to psychiatrists, the fear of public speaking is caused by the fear of ostracism, the fear of standing out, the fear of criticism, the fear of ridicule, the fear of being an outcast. The fear of being different prevents most people from seeking new ways to solve their problems.

That is why my educated dad said the Japanese valued the power of the mirror the most, for it is only when we as humans look into the mirror do we find truth. And the main reason that most people say "Play it safe" is out of fear. That goes for anything, be it sports, relationships, career, money.

It is that same fear, the fear of ostracism that causes people to conform and not question commonly accepted opinions or popular trends. "Your home is an asset." "Get a bill consolidation loan and get out of debt." "Work harder." "It's a promotion." "Someday I'll be a vice president." "Save money." "When I get a raise, I'll buy us a bigger house." "Mutual funds are safe." "Tickle Me Elmo dolls are out of stock, but I just happen to have one in back that another customer has not come by for yet."

Many great financial problems are caused by going along with the crowd and trying to keep up with the Joneses. Occasionally, we all need to look in the mirror and be true to our inner wisdom rather than our fears.

By the time Mike and I were 16 years old, we began to have problems in school. We were not bad kids. We just began to separate from the crowd. We worked for Mike's dad after school and on the weekends. Mike and I often spent hours after work just sitting at a table with his dad while he held meetings with his bankers, attorneys, accountants, brokers, investors, managers and employees. Here was a man who had left school at the age of 13, now directing, instructing, ordering and asking questions of educated people. They came at his beck and call, and cringed when he did not approve of them.

Here was a man who had not gone along with the crowd. He was a man who did his own thinking and detested the words, "We have to do it this way because that's the way everyone else does it." He also hated the word "can't." If you wanted him to do something, just say, "I don't think you can do it."

Mike and I learned more sitting at his meetings than we did in all our years of school, college included. Mike's dad was not school educated, but he was financially educated and successful as a result. He use to tell us over and over again. "An intelligent person hires people who are more intelligent than they are." So Mike and I had the benefit of spending hours listening to and, in the process, learning from intelligent people.

But because of this, both Mike and I just could not go along with the standard dogma that our teachers preached. And that caused the problems. Whenever the teacher said, "If you don't get good grades, you won't do well in the real world," Mike and I just raised our eyebrows. When we were told to follow set procedures and not deviate from the rules, we could see how this schooling process actually discouraged creativity. We started to understand why our rich dad told us that schools were designed to produce good employees instead of employers.

Occasionally Mike or I would ask our teachers how what we studied was applicable, or we asked why we never studied money and how it worked. To the later question, we often got the answer that money was not important, that if we excelled in our education, the money would follow.

The more we knew about the power of money, the more distant we grew from the teachers and our classmates.

My highly educated dad never pressured me about my grades. I often wondered why. But we did begin to argue about money. By the time I was 16, I probably had a far better foundation with money than both my mom and dad. I could keep books, I listened to tax accountants, corporate attorneys, bankers, real estate brokers, investors and so forth. My dad talked to teachers.

One day, my dad was telling me why our home was his greatest investment. A not-too-pleasant argument took place when I showed him why I thought a house was not a good investment.

The following diagram illustrates the difference in perception between my rich dad and my poor dad when it came to their homes. One dad thought his house was an asset, and the other dad thought it was a liability.

Rich Dad

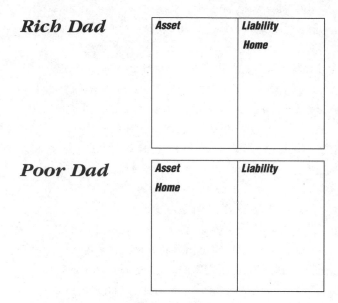

I remember when I drew the following diagram for my dad showing him the direction of cash flow. I also showed him the ancillary expenses that went along with owning the home. A bigger home meant bigger expenses, and the cash flow kept going out through the expense column.

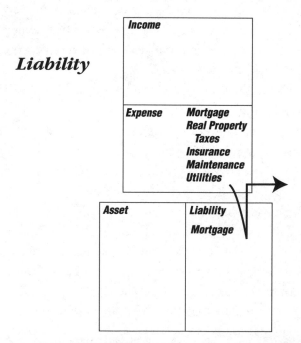

Today, I am still challenged on the idea of a house not being an asset. And I know that for many people, it is their dream as well as their largest investment. And owning your own home is better than nothing. I simply offer an alternate way of looking at this popular dogma. If my wife and I were to buy a bigger, more flashy house we realize it would not be an asset, it would be a liability, since it would take money out of our pocket.

So here is the argument I put forth. I really do not expect most people to agree with it because a nice home is an emotional thing. And when it comes to money, high emotions tend to lower financial intelligence. I know from personal experience that money has a way of making every decision emotional.

1. When it comes to houses, I point out that most people work all their lives paying for a home they never own. In other words, most people buy a new house every so many years, each time incurring a new 30-year loan to pay off the previous one.

2. Even though people receive a tax deduction for interest on mortgage payments, they pay for all their other expenses with after-tax dollars. Even after they pay off their mortgage.

3. Property taxes. My wife's parents were shocked when the property taxes on their home went to $1,000 a month. This was after they had retired, so the increase put a strain on their retirement budget, and they felt forced to move.

4. Houses do not always go up in value. In 1997, I still have friends who owe a million dollars for a home that will today sell for only $700,000.

5. The greatest losses of all are those from missed opportunities. If all your money is tied up in your house, you may be forced to work harder because your money continues blowing out of the expense column, instead of adding to the asset column, the classic middle class cash flow pattern. If a young couple would put more money into their asset column early on, their later years would get easier, especially as they prepared to send their children to college. Their assets would have grown and would be available to help cover expenses. All too often, a house only serves as a vehicle for incurring a home-equity loan to pay for mounting expenses.

In summary, the end result in making a decision to own a house that is too expensive in lieu of starting an investment portfolio early on impacts an individual in at least the following three ways:

1. Loss of time, during which other assets could have grown in value.
2. Loss of additional capital, which could have been invested instead of paying for high-maintenance expenses related directly to the home.
3. Loss of education. Too often, people count their house, savings and retirement plan as all they have in their asset column. Because they have no money to invest, they simply do not invest. This costs them investment experience. Most never become what the investment world calls a "sophisticated investor." And the best investments are usually first sold to "sophisticated investors," who then turn around and sell them to the people playing it safe.

My educated dad's personal financial statement best demonstrates the life of someone in the rat race. His expenses seem to always keep up with his income, never allowing him to invest in assets. As a result, his liabilities, such as his mortgage and credit card debts are larger than his assets. The following picture is worth a thousand words:

Educated Dad's Financial Statement

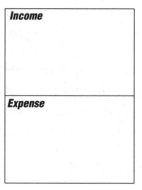

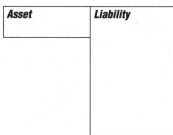

My rich dad's personal financial statement, on the other hand, reflects the results of a life dedicated to investing and minimizing liabilities:

Rich Dad's Financial Statement

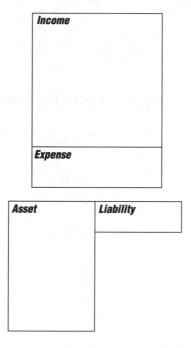

A review of my rich dad's financial statement is why the rich get richer. The asset column generates more than enough income to cover expenses, with the balance reinvested into the asset column. The asset column continues to grow and, therefore, the income it produces grows with it.

The result being: The rich get richer!

Why the Rich Get Richer

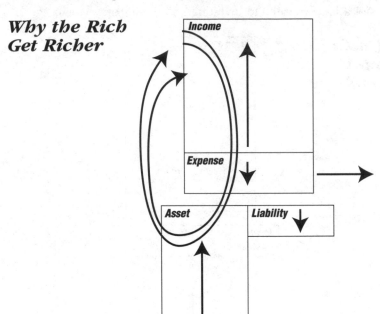

The middle class finds itself in a constant state of financial struggle. Their primary income is through wages, and as their wages increase, so do their taxes. Their expenses tend to increase in equal increments as their wages increase; hence the phrase "the rat race." They treat their home as their primary asset, instead on investing in income-producing assets.

Why the Middle Class Struggle

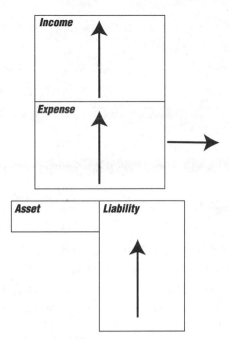

This pattern of treating your home as an investment and the philosophy that a pay raise means you can buy a larger home or spend more is the foundation of today's debt-ridden society. This process of increased spending throws families into greater debt and into more financial uncertainty, even though they may be advancing in their jobs and receiving pay raises on a regular basis. This is high risk living caused by weak financial education.

The massive loss of jobs in the 1990s—the downsizing of businesses—has brought to light how shaky the middle class really is financially. Suddenly, company pension plans are being replaced by 401k plans. Social Security is obviously in trouble and cannot be looked at as a source for retirement. Panic has set in for the middle class. The good thing today is that many of these people have recognized these issues and have begun buying mutual funds. This increase in investing is largely responsible for the huge rally we have seen in the stock market. Today, there are more and more mutual funds being created to answer the demand by the middle class.

Mutual funds are popular because they represent safety. Average mutual fund buyers are too busy working to pay taxes and mortgages, save for their children's college and pay off credit cards. They do not have time to study to learn how to invest, so they rely on the expertise of the manager of a mutual fund. Also, because the mutual fund includes many different types of investments, they feel their money is safer because it is "diversified."

This group of educated middle class subscribes to the "diversify" dogma put out by mutual fund brokers and financial planners. Play it safe. Avoid risk.

The real tragedy is that the lack of early financial education is what creates the risk faced by average middle class people. The reason they have to play it safe is because their financial positions are tenuous at best. Their balance sheets are not balanced. They are loaded with liabilities, with no real assets that generate income. Typically, their only source of income is their paycheck. Their livelihood becomes entirely dependent on their employer.

So when genuine "deals of a lifetime" come along, those same people cannot take advantage of the opportunity. They must play it safe, simply because they are working so hard, are taxed to the max, and are loaded with debt.

As I said at the start of this section, the most important rule is to know the difference between an asset and a liability. Once you understand the difference, concentrate your efforts on only buying income-generating assets. That's the best way to get started on a path to becoming rich. Keep doing that, and your asset column will grow. Focus on keeping liabilities and expenses down. This will make more money available to continue pouring into the asset column. Soon, the asset base will be so deep that you can afford to look at more speculative investments. Investments that may have returns of 100 percent to infinity. Investments that for $5,000 are soon turned into $1 million or more. Investments that the middle class calls "too risky." The investment is not risky. It's the lack of simple financial intelligence, beginning with financial literacy, that causes the individual to be "too risky."

If you do what the masses do, you get the following picture.

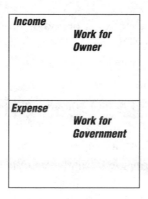

Income	
	Work for Owner
Expense	
	Work for Government

Asset	Liability
	Work for Bank

As an employee who is also a homeowner, your working efforts are generally as follows:

1. You work for someone else. Most people, working for a paycheck, are making the owner, or the shareholders richer. Your efforts and success will help provide for the owner's success and retirement.

2. You work for the government. The government takes its share from your paycheck before you even see it. By working harder, you simply increase the amount of taxes taken by the government — most people work from January to May just for the government.

3. You work for the bank. After taxes, your next largest expense is usually your mortgage and credit card debt.

The problem with simply working harder is that each of these three levels takes a greater share of your increased efforts. You need to learn how to have your increased efforts benefit you and your family directly.

Once you have decided to concentrate on minding your own business, how do you set your goals? For most people, they must keep their profession and rely on their wages to fund their acquisition of assets.

As their assets grow, how do they measure the extent of their success? When does someone realize that they are rich, that they have wealth? As well as having my own definitions for assets and liabilities, I also have my own definition for wealth. Actually I borrowed it from a man named Buckminster Fuller. Some call him a quack, and others call him a living genius. Years ago he got all the architects buzzing because he applied for a patent in 1961 for something called a geodesic dome. But in the application, Fuller also said something about wealth. It was pretty confusing at first, but after reading it for awhile, it began to make some sense: Wealth is a person's ability to survive so many number of days forward... or if I stopped working today, how long could I survive?

Unlike net worth—the difference between your assets and liabilities, which is often filled with a person's expensive junk and opinions of what things are worth—this definition creates the possibility for developing a truly accurate measurement. I could now measure and really know where I was in terms of my goal to become financially independent.

Although net worth often includes these non-cash-producing assets, like stuff you bought that now sits in your garage, wealth measures how much money your money is making and, therefore, your financial survivability.

Wealth is the measure of the cash flow from the asset column compared with the expense column.

Let's use an example. Let's say I have cash flow from my asset column of $1,000 a month. And I have monthly expenses of $2,000. What is my wealth?

Let's go back to Buckminster Fuller's definition. Using his definition, how many days forward can I survive? And let's assume a 30-day month. By that definition, I have enough cash flow for half a month.

When I have achieved $2,000 a month cash flow from my assets, then I will be wealthy.

So I am not yet rich, but I am wealthy. I now have income generated from assets each month that fully cover my monthly expenses. If I want to increase my expenses, I first must increase my cash flow from assets to maintain this level of wealth. Take notice that it is at this point that I no longer am dependent on my wages. I have focused on and been successful in building an asset column that has made me financially independent. If I quit my job today, I would be able to cover my monthly expenses with the cash flow from my assets.

My next goal would be to have the excess cash flow from my assets reinvested into the asset column. The more money that goes into my asset column, the more my asset column grows. The more my assets grow, the more my cash flow grows. And as long as I keep my expenses less than the cash flow from these assets, I will grow richer, with more and more income from sources other than my physical labor.

As this reinvestment process continues, I am well on my way to being rich. The actual definition of rich is in the eye of the beholder. You can never be too rich.

Just remember this simple observation:

The rich buy assets.

The poor only have expenses.

The middle class buys liabilities they think are assets.

So how do I start minding my own business? What is the answer? Listen to the founder of McDonald's.

MIND YOUR OWN BUSINESS

CHAPTER FOUR
Lesson Three:

Mind Your Own Business

*I*n 1974, Ray Kroc, the founder of McDonald's, was asked to speak to the MBA class at the University of Texas at Austin. A dear friend of mine, Keith Cunningham, was a student in that MBA class. After a powerful and inspiring talk, the class adjourned and the students asked Ray if he would join them at their favorite hangout to have a few beers. Ray graciously accepted.

"What business am I in?" Ray asked, once the group had all their beers in hand.

"Everyone laughed," said Keith. "Most of the MBA students thought Ray was just fooling around."

No one answered, so Ray asked the question again. "What business do you think I'm in?"

The students laughed again, and finally one brave soul yelled out, "Ray, who in the world does not know that you're in the hamburger business."

Ray chuckled. "That is what I thought you would say." He paused and then quickly said, "Ladies and gentlemen, I'm not in the hamburger business. My business is real estate."

Keith said that Ray spent a good amount of time explaining his viewpoint. In their business plan, Ray knew that the primary business focus was to sell hamburger franchises, but what he never lost sight of was the location of each franchise. He knew that the real estate and its location was the most significant factor in the success of each franchise. Basically, the person that bought the franchise was also paying for, buying, the land under the franchise for Ray Kroc's organization.

McDonald's today is the largest single owner of real estate in the world, owning even more than the Catholic Church. Today, McDonald's owns some of the most valuable intersections and street corners in America, as well as in other parts of the world.

Keith said it was one of the most important lessons in his life. Today, Keith owns car washes, but his business is the real estate under those car washes.

The previous chapter ended with the diagrams illustrating that most people work for everyone else but themselves. They work first for the owners of the company, then for the government through taxes, and finally for the bank that owns their mortgage.

As a young boy, we did not have a McDonald's nearby. Yet, my rich dad was responsible for teaching Mike and me the same lesson that Ray Kroc talked about at the University of Texas. It is secret No. 3 of the rich.

The secret is: "Mind your own business." Financial struggle is often directly the result of people working all their life for someone else. Many people will have nothing at the end of their working days.

Again, a picture is worth a thousand words. Here is a diagram of the income statement and balance sheet that best describes Ray Kroc's advice:

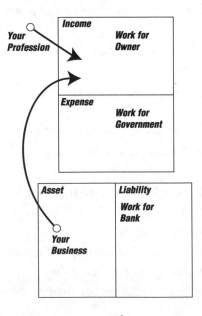

Our current educational system focuses on preparing today's youth to get good jobs by developing scholastic skills. Their lives will revolve around their wages, or as described earlier, their income column. And after developing scholastic skills, they go on to higher levels of schooling to enhance their professional abilities. They study to become engineers, scientists, cooks, police officers, artists, writers and so on. These professional skills allow them to enter the workforce and work for money.

There is a big difference between your profession and your business. Often I ask people, "What is your business?" And they will say, "Oh I'm a banker." Then I ask them if they own the bank? And they usually respond. "No, I work there."

In that instance, they have confused their profession with their business. Their profession may be a banker, but they still need their own business. Ray Kroc was clear on the difference between his profession and his business. His profession was always the same. He was a salesman. At one time he sold mixers for milkshakes, and soon thereafter he was selling hamburger franchises. But while his profession was selling hamburger franchises, his business was the accumulation of income-producing real estate.

A problem with school is that you often become what you study. So if you study, say, cooking, you become a chef. If you study the law, you become an attorney, and a study of auto mechanics makes you a mechanic. The mistake in becoming what you study is that too many people forget to mind their own business. They spend their lives minding someone else's business and making that person rich.

To become financially secure, a person needs to mind their own business. Your business revolves around your asset column, as opposed to your income column. As stated earlier, the No. 1 rule is to know the difference between an asset and a liability, and to buy assets. The rich focus on their asset columns while everyone else focuses on their income statements.

That is why we hear so often: "I need a raise." "If only I had a promotion." "I am going to go back to school to get more training so I can get a better job." "I am going to work overtime." "Maybe I can get a second job." "I'm quitting in two weeks. I found a job that pays more."

In some circles, these are sensible ideas. Yet, if you listen to Ray Kroc, you are still not minding your own business. These ideas all still focus on the income column and will only help a person become more financially secure if the additional money is used to purchase income-generating assets.

The primary reason the majority of the poor and middle class are fiscally conservative—which means, "I can't afford to take risks"—is that they have no financial foundation. They have to cling to their jobs. They have to play it safe.

When downsizing became the "in" thing to do, millions of workers found out their largest so-called asset, their home, was eating them alive. Their asset, called a house, still cost them money every month. Their car, another "asset," was eating them alive. The golf clubs in the garage that cost $1,000 were not worth $1,000 anymore. Without job security, they had nothing to fall back on. What they thought were assets could not help them survive in a time of financial crisis.

I assume most of us have filled out a credit application for a banker to buy a house or to buy a car. It is always interesting to look at the "net worth" section. It is interesting because of what accepted banking and accounting practices allow a person to count as assets.

One day, to get a loan, my financial position did not look too good. So I added my new golf clubs, my art collection, books, stereo, television, Armani suits, wristwatches, shoes and other personal effects to boost the number in the asset column.

But I was turned down for the loan because I had too much investment real estate. The loan committee did not like that I made so much money off of apartment houses. They wanted to know why I did not have a normal job, with a salary. They did not question the Armani suits, golf clubs or art collection. Life is sometimes tough when you do not fit the "standard" profile.

I cringe every time I hear someone say to me that their net worth is a million dollars or $100,000 dollars or whatever. One of the main reasons net worth is not accurate is simply because the moment you begin selling your assets, you are taxed for any gains.

So many people have put themselves in deep financial trouble when they run short of income. To raise cash, they sell their assets. First, their personal assets can generally be sold for only a fraction of the value that is listed in their personal balance sheet. Or if there is a gain on the sale of the assets, they are taxed on the gain. So again, the government takes its share of the gain, thus reducing the amount available to help them out of debt. That is why I say someone's net worth is often "worth less" than they think.

Start minding your own business. Keep your daytime job, but start buying real assets, not liabilities or personal effects that have no real value once you get them home. A new car loses nearly 25 percent of the price you pay for it the moment you drive it off the lot. It is not a true asset even if your banker lets you list it as one. My $400 new titanium driver was worth $150 the moment I teed off.

For adults, keep your expenses low, reduce your liabilities and diligently build a base of solid assets. For young people who have not yet left home, it is important for parents to teach them the difference between an asset and a liability. Get them to start building a solid asset column before they leave home, get married, buy a house, have kids and get stuck in a risky financial position, clinging to a job and buying everything on credit. I see so many young couples who get married and trap themselves into a lifestyle that will not let them get out of debt for most of their working years.

For most people, just as the last child leaves home, the parents realize they have not adequately prepared for retirement and they begin to scramble to put some money away. Then, their own parents become ill and they find themselves with new responsibilities.

So what kind of assets am I suggesting that you or your children acquire? In my world, real assets fall into several different categories:

1. Businesses that do not require my presence. I own them, but they are managed or run by other people. If I have to work there, it's not a business. It becomes my job.
2. Stocks.
3. Bonds.
4. Mutual funds.
5. Income-generating real estate.
6. Notes (IOUs).
7. Royalties from intellectual property such as music, scripts, patents.
8. And anything else that has value, produces income or appreciates and has a ready market.

As a young boy, my educated dad encouraged me to find a safe job. My rich dad, on the other hand, encouraged me to begin acquiring assets that I loved. "If you don't love it, you won't take care of it." I collect real estate simply because I love buildings and land. I love shopping for them. I could look at them all day long. When problems arise, the problems are not so bad that it changes my love for real estate. For people who hate real estate, they shouldn't buy it.

I love stocks of small companies, especially startups. The reason is that I am an entrepreneur, not a corporate person. In my early years, I worked in large organizations, such as Standard Oil of California, the U.S. Marine Corps, and Xerox Corp. I enjoyed my time with those organizations and have fond memories, but I know deep down I am not a company man. I like starting companies, not running them. So my stock buys are usually of small companies, and sometimes I even start the company and take it public. Fortunes are made in new-stock issues, and I love the game. Many people are afraid of small-cap companies and call them risky, and they are. But risk is always diminished if you love what the investment is, understand it and know the game. With small companies, my investment strategy is to be out of the stock in a year. My real estate strategy, on the other hand, is to start small and keep trading the properties up for bigger properties and, therefore, delaying paying taxes on the gain. This allows the value to increase dramatically. I generally hold real estate less than seven years.

For years, even while I was with the Marine Corps and Xerox, I did what my rich dad recommended. I kept my daytime job, but I still minded my own business. I was active in my asset column. I traded real estate and small stocks. Rich dad always stressed the importance of financial literacy. The better I was at understanding the accounting and cash management, the better I would be at analyzing investments and eventually starting and building my own company.

I would not encourage anyone to start a company unless they really want to. Knowing what I know about running a company, I would not wish that task on anyone. There are times when people cannot find employment, where starting a company is a solution for them. The odds are against success: Nine out of 10 companies fail in five years. Of those that survive the first five years, nine out of every 10 of those eventually fail, as well. So only if you really have the desire to own your own company do I recommend it. Otherwise, keep your daytime job and mind your own business.

When I say mind your own business, I mean to build and keep your asset column strong. Once a dollar goes into it, never let it come out. Think of it this way, once a dollar goes into your asset column, it becomes your employee. The best thing about money is that it works 24 hours a day and can work for generations. Keep your daytime job, be a great hard-working employee, but keep building that asset column.

As your cash flow grows, you can buy some luxuries. An important distinction is that rich people buy luxuries last, while the poor and middle class tend to buy luxuries first. The poor and the middle class often buy luxury items such as big houses, diamonds, furs, jewelry or boats because they want to look rich. They look rich, but in reality they just get deeper in debt on credit. The old-money people, the long-term rich, built their asset column first. Then, the income generated from the asset column bought their luxuries. The poor and middle class buy luxuries with their own sweat, blood and children's inheritance.

A true luxury is a reward for investing in and developing a real asset. For example, when my wife and I had extra money coming from our apartment houses, she went out and bought her Mercedes. It did not take any extra work or risk on her part because the apartment house bought the car. She did, however, have to wait for it for four years while the real estate investment portfolio grew and finally began throwing off enough extra cash flow to pay for the car. But the luxury, the Mercedes, was a true reward because she had proved she knew how to grow her asset column. That car now means a lot more to her than simply another pretty car. It means she used her financial intelligence to afford it.

What most people do is they impulsively go out and buy a new car, or some other luxury, on credit. They may feel bored and just want a new toy. Buying a luxury on credit often causes a person to sooner or later actually resent that luxury because the debt on the luxury becomes a financial burden.

After you've taken the time and invested in and built your own business, you are now ready to add the magic touch—the biggest secret of the rich. The secret that puts the rich way ahead of the pack. The reward at the end of the road for diligently taking the time to mind your own business.

THE HISTORY OF TAXES AND THE POWER OF CORPORATIONS

The History of Taxes and The Power of Corporations

I remember in school being told the story of Robin Hood and his Merry Men. My schoolteacher thought it was a wonderful story of a romantic hero, a Kevin Costner type, who robbed from the rich and gave to the poor. My rich dad did not see Robin Hood as a hero. He called Robin Hood a crook.

Robin Hood may be long gone, but his followers live on. How often I still hear people say, "Why don't the rich pay for it?" Or "The rich should pay more in taxes and give it to the poor."

It is this idea of Robin Hood, or taking from the rich to give to the poor that has caused the most pain for the poor and the middle class. The reason the middle class is so heavily taxed is because of the Robin Hood ideal. The real reality is that the rich are not taxed. It's the middle class who pays for the poor, especially the educated upper-income middle class.

Again, to understand fully how things happen, we need to look at the historical perspective. We need to look at the history of taxes. Although my highly educated dad was an expert on the history of education, my rich dad fashioned himself as an expert on the history of taxes.

Rich dad explained to Mike and me that in England and America originally, there were no taxes. Occasionally there were temporary taxes levied in order to pay for wars. The king or the president would put the word out and ask everyone to "chip in." Taxes were levied in Britain for the fight against Napoleon from 1799 to 1816, and in America taxes were levied to pay for the Civil War from 1861 to 1865.

In 1874, England made income tax a permanent levy on its citizens. In 1913, an income tax became permanent in the United States with the adoption of the 16th Amendment to the Constitution. At one time, Americans were anti-tax. It had been the excessive tax on tea that led to the famous Tea Party in Boston Harbor, an incident that helped ignite the Revolutionary War. It took approximately 50 years in both England and the United States to sell the idea of a regular income tax.

What these historical dates fail to reveal is that both of these taxes were initially levied against only the rich. It was this point that rich dad wanted Mike and me to understand. He explained that the idea of taxes was made popular, and accepted by the majority, by telling the poor and the middle class that taxes were created only to punish the rich. This is how the masses voted for the law, and it became constitutionally legal. Although it was intended to punish the rich, in reality it wound up punishing the very people who voted for it, the poor and middle class.

"Once government got a taste of money, the appetite grew," said rich dad. "Your dad and I are exactly opposite. He's a government bureaucrat, and I am a capitalist. We get paid, and our success is measured on opposite behaviors. He gets paid to spend money and hire people. The more he spends and the more people he hires, the larger his organization becomes. In the government, the larger his organization, the more he is respected. On the other hand, within my organization, the fewer people I hire and the less money I spend, the more I am respected by my investors. That's why I don't like government people. They have different objectives from most business people. As the government grows, more and more tax dollars will be needed to support it."

My educated dad sincerely believed that government should help people. He loved John F. Kennedy and especially the idea of the Peace Corps. He loved the idea so much that both he and my mom worked for the Peace Corps training volunteers to go to Malaysia, Thailand and the Philippines. He always strived for additional grants and increases in his budget so he could hire more people, both in his job with the Education Department and in the Peace Corps. That was his job.

From the time I was about 10 years old, I would hear from my rich dad that government workers were a pack of lazy thieves, and from my poor dad I would hear how the rich were greedy crooks who should be made to pay more taxes. Both sides have valid points. It was difficult to go to work for one of the biggest capitalists in town and come home to a father who was a prominent government leader. It was not easy knowing who to believe.

Yet, when you study the history of taxes, an interesting perspective emerges. As I said, the passage of taxes was only possible because the masses believed in the Robin Hood theory of economics, which was to take from the rich and give to everyone else. The problem was that the government's appetite for money was so great that taxes soon needed to be levied on the middle class, and from there it kept "trickling down."

The rich, on the other hand, saw an opportunity. They do not play by the same set of rules. As I've stated, the rich already knew about corporations, which became popular in the days of sailing ships. The rich created the corporation as a vehicle to limit their risk to the assets of each voyage. The rich put their money into a corporation to finance the voyage. The corporation would then hire a crew to sail to the New World to look for treasures. If the ship was lost, the crew lost their lives, but the loss to the rich would be limited only to the money they invested for that particular voyage. The diagram that follows shows how the corporate structure sits outside your personal income statement and balance sheet.

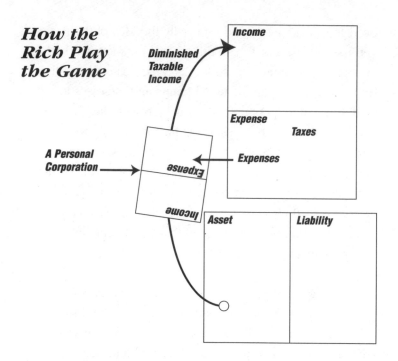

How the Rich Play the Game

Diminished Taxable Income

Income

A Personal Corporation

Expense

Income

Expense

Taxes

Expenses

Asset

Liability

It is the knowledge of the power of the legal structure of the corporation that really gives the rich a vast advantage over the poor and the middle class. Having two fathers teaching me, one a socialist and the other a capitalist, I quickly began to realize that the philosophy of the capitalist made more financial sense to me. It seemed to me that the socialists ultimately penalized themselves, due to their lack of financial education. No matter what the "Take from the rich" crowd came up with, the rich always found a way to outsmart them. That is how taxes were eventually levied on the middle class. The rich outsmarted the intellectuals, solely because they understood the power of money, a subject not taught in schools.

How did the rich outsmart the intellectuals? Once the "Take from the rich" tax was passed, cash started flowing into government coffers. Initially, people were happy. Money was handed out to government workers and the rich. It went to government workers in the form of jobs and pensions. It went to the rich via their factories receiving government contracts. The government became a large pool of money, but the problem was the fiscal management of that money. There really is no recirculation. In other words, the government policy, if you were a government bureaucrat, was to avoid having excess money. If you failed to spend your allotted funding, you risked losing it in the next budget.

You would certainly not be recognized for being efficient. Business people, on the other hand, are rewarded for having excess money and are recognized for their efficiency.

As this cycle of growing government spending continued, the demand for money increased and the "Tax the rich" idea was now being adjusted to include lower-income levels, down to the very people who voted it in, the poor and the middle class.

True capitalists used their financial knowledge to simply find a way to escape. They headed back to the protection of a corporation. A corporation protects the rich. But what many people who have never formed a corporation do not know is that a corporation is not really a thing. A corporation is merely a file folder with some legal documents in it, sitting in some attorney's office registered with a state government agency. It's not a big building with the name of the corporation on it. It's not a factory or a group of people. A corporation is merely a legal document that creates a legal body without a soul. The wealth of the rich was once again protected. Once again, the use of corporations became popular—once the permanent income laws were passed—because the income-tax rate of the corporation was less than the individual income-tax rates. In addition, as described earlier, certain expenses could be paid with pre-tax dollars within the corporation.

This war between the haves and have-nots has been going on for hundreds of years. It is the "Take from the rich" crowd versus the rich. The battle is waged whenever and wherever laws are made. The battle will go on forever. The problem is, the people who lose are the uninformed. The ones who get up every day and diligently go to work and pay taxes. If they only understood the way the rich play the game, they could play it too. Then, they would be on their way to their own financial independence. This is why I cringe every time I hear a parent advise their children to go to school, so they can find a safe, secure job. An employee with a safe, secure job, without financial aptitude, has no escape.

Average Americans today work five to six months for the government before they make enough to cover their taxes. In my opinion, that is a long time. The harder you work, the more you pay the government. That is why I believe that the idea of "Take from the rich" backfired on the very people who voted it in.

Every time people try to punish the rich, the rich don't simply comply, they react. They have the money, power and intent to change things. They do not just sit there and voluntarily pay more taxes. They search for ways to minimize their tax burden. They hire smart attorneys and accountants, and persuade politicians to change laws or create legal loopholes. They have the resources to effect change.

The Tax Code of the United States also allows other ways to save on taxes. Most of these vehicles are available to anyone, but it is the rich who usually look for them because they are minding their own business. For example, "1031" is jargon for Section 1031 of the Internal Revenue Code, which allows a seller to delay paying taxes on a piece of real estate that is sold for a capital gain through an exchange for a more expensive piece of real estate. Real estate is one investment vehicle that allows such a great tax advantage. As long as you keep trading up in value, you will not be taxed on the gains, until you liquidate. People who do not take advantage of these tax savings offered legally are missing a great opportunity to build their asset columns.

The poor and middle class do not have the same resources. They sit there and let the government's needles enter their arm and allow the blood donation to begin. Today, I am constantly shocked at the number of people who pay more taxes, or take fewer deductions, simply because they are afraid of the government. And I do know how frightening and intimidating a government tax agent can be. I have had friends who have had their businesses shut down and destroyed, only to find out it was a mistake on the part of the government. I realize all that. But the price of working from January to mid-May is a high price to pay for that intimidation. My poor dad never fought back. My rich dad didn't either. He just played the game smarter, and he did it through corporations—the biggest secret of the rich.

You may remember the first lesson I learned from my rich dad. I was a little boy of 9 who had to sit and wait for him to choose to talk to me. I often sat in his office waiting for him to "get to me." He was ignoring me on purpose. He wanted me to recognize his power and desire to have that power for myself one day. For all the years I studied and learned from him, he always reminded me that knowledge was power. And with money comes great power that requires the right knowledge to keep it and make it multiply. Without that knowledge, the world pushes you around. Rich dad constantly reminded Mike and me that the biggest bully was not the boss or the supervisor, but the tax man. The tax man will always take more if you let him.

The first lesson of having money work for me, as opposed to working for money, is really all about power. If you work for money, you give the power up to your employer. If your money works for you, you keep and control the power.

Once we had this knowledge of the power of money working for us, he wanted us to be financially smart and not let bullies push us around. You need to know the law and how the system works. If you're ignorant, it is easy to be bullied. If you know what you're talking about, you have a fighting chance. That is why he paid so much for smart tax accountants and attorneys. It was less expensive to pay them than pay the government. His best lesson to me, which I have used most of my life, is "Be smart and you won't be pushed around as much." He knew the law because he was a law-abiding citizen. He knew the law because it was expensive to not know the law. "If you know you're right, you're not afraid of fighting back." Even if you are taking on Robin Hood and his band of Merry Men.

My highly educated dad always encouraged me to seek a good job with a strong corporation. He spoke of the virtues of "working your way up the corporate ladder." He didn't understand that, by relying solely on a paycheck from a corporate employer, I would be a docile cow ready for milking.

When I told my rich dad of my father's advice, he only chuckled. "Why not own the ladder?" was all he said.

As a young boy, I did not understand what rich dad meant by owning my own corporation. It was an idea that seemed impossible, and intimidating. Although I was excited by the idea, my youth would not let me envision the possibility that grownups would someday work for a company I would own.

The point is, if not for my rich dad, I would have probably followed my educated dad's advice. It was merely the occasional reminder of my rich dad that kept the idea of owning my own corporation alive and kept me on a different path. By the time I was 15 or 16, I knew I was not going to continue down the path my educated dad was recommending. I did not know how I was going to do it, but I was determined not to head in the direction most of my classmates were heading. That decision changed my life.

It was not until I was in my mid-20s that my rich dad's advice began to make more sense. I was just out of the Marine Corps and working for Xerox. I was making a lot of money, but every time I looked at my paycheck, I was always disappointed. The deductions were so large, and the more I worked, the greater the deductions. As I became more successful, my bosses talked about promotions and raises. It was flattering, but I could hear my rich dad asking me in my ear: "Who are you working for? Who are you making rich?"

In 1974, while still an employee for Xerox, I formed my first corporation and began "minding my own business." There were already a few assets in my asset column, but now I was determined to focus on making it bigger. Those paychecks with all the deductions made all the years of my rich dad's advice make total sense. I could see the future if I followed my educated dad's advice.

Many employers feel that advising their workers to mind their own business is bad for business. I am sure it can be for certain individuals. But for me, focusing on my own business, developing assets, made me a better employee. I now had a purpose. I came in early and worked diligently, amassing as much money as possible so I could begin investing in real estate. Hawaii was just set to boom, and there were fortunes to be made. The more I realized we were in the beginning stages of a boom, the more Xerox machines I sold. The more I sold, the more money I made, and, of course, the more deductions there were from my paycheck. It was inspiring. I wanted out of the trap of being an employee so badly that I worked harder, not less. By 1978, I was consistently one of the top five salespeople in sales, often No. 1. I badly wanted out of the rat race.

In less than three years, I was making more in my own little corporation, which was a real estate holding company, than I was making at Xerox. And the money I was making in my asset column, in my own corporation, was money working for me. Not me pounding on doors selling copiers. My rich dad's advice made much more sense. Soon the cash flow from my properties was so strong that my company bought me my first Porsche. My fellow Xerox salespeople thought I was spending my commissions. I wasn't. I was investing my commissions in assets.

My money was working hard to make more money. Each dollar in my asset column was a great employee, working hard to make more employees and buy the boss a new Porsche with before-tax dollars. I began to work harder for Xerox. The plan was working, and my Porsche was the proof.

By using the lessons I learned from my rich dad, I was able to get out of the "proverbial rat race" of being an employee at an early age. It was made possible because of the strong financial knowledge I had acquired through these lessons. Without this financial knowledge, which I call financial IQ, my road to financial independence would have been much more difficult. I now teach others through financial seminars in the hope that I may share my knowledge with them. Whenever I do my talks, I remind people that financial IQ is made up of knowledge from four broad areas of expertise.

No. 1 is accounting. What I call financial literacy. A vital skill if you want to build an empire. The more money you are responsible for, the more accuracy is required, or the house comes tumbling down. This is the left brain side, or the details. Financial literacy is the ability to read and understand financial statements. This ability allows you to identify the strengths and weaknesses of any business.

No. 2 is investing. What I call the science of money making money. This involves strategies and formulas. This is the right brain side, or the creative side.

No. 3 is understanding markets. The science of supply and demand. There is a need to know the "technical" aspects of the market, which is emotion driven; the Tickle Me Elmo doll during Christmas 1996 is a case of a technical or emotion-driven market. The other market factor is the "fundamental" or the economic sense of an investment. Does an investment make sense or does it not make sense based on the current market conditions.

Many people think the concepts of investing and understanding the market are too complex for kids. They fail to see that kids know those subjects intuitively. For those not familiar with the Elmo doll, it was a Sesame Street character that was highly touted to the kids just before Christmas. Most all kids wanted one, and put it at the top of their Christmas list. Many parents wondered if the company intentionally held the product off the market, while continuing to advertise it for Christmas. A panic set in due to high demand and lack of supply. Having no dolls to buy in the stores, scalpers saw an opportunity to make a small fortune from desperate parents. The unlucky parents who did not find a doll were forced to buy another toy for Christmas. The incredible popularity of the Tickle Me Elmo doll made no sense to me, but it serves as an excellent example of supply and demand economics. The same thing goes on in the stock, bond, real estate and baseball-card markets.

No. 4 is the law. For instance, utilizing a corporation wrapped around the technical skills of accounting, investing and markets can aid explosive growth. An individual with the knowledge of the tax advantages and protection provided by a corporation can get rich so much faster than someone who is an employee or a small-business sole proprietor. It's like the difference between someone walking and someone flying. The difference is profound when it comes to long-term wealth.

1. Tax advantages: A corporation can do so many things that an individual cannot. Like pay for expenses before it pays taxes. That is a whole area of expertise that is so exciting, but not necessary to get into unless you have sizable assets or a business.

Employees earn and get taxed and they try to live on what is left. A corporation earns, spends everything it can, and is taxed on anything that is left. It's one of the biggest legal tax loopholes that the rich use. They're easy to set up and are not expensive if you own investments that are producing good cash flow. For example; by owning your own corporation — vacations are board meetings in Hawaii. Car payments, insurance, repairs are company expenses. Health club membership is a company expense. Most restaurant meals are partial expenses. And on and on — but do it legally with pre-tax dollars.

2. Protection from lawsuits. We live in a litigious society. Everybody wants a piece of your action. The rich hide much of their wealth using vehicles such as corporations and trusts to protect their assets from creditors. When someone sues a wealthy individual they are often met with layers of legal protection, and often find that the wealthy person actually owns nothing. They control everything, but own nothing. The poor and middle class try to own everything and lose it to the government or to fellow citizens who like to sue the rich. They learned it from the Robin Hood story. Take from the rich, give to the poor.

It is not the purpose of this book to go into the specifics of owning a corporation. But I will say that if you own any kind of legitimate assets, I would consider finding out more about the benefits and protection offered by a corporation as soon as possible. There are many books written on the subject that will detail the benefits and even walk you through the steps necessary to set up a corporation. One book in particular, *Inc. and Grow Rich* provides a wonderful insight into the power of personal corporations.

Financial IQ is actually the synergy of many skills and talents. But I would say it is the combination of the four technical skills listed above that make up basic financial intelligence. If you aspire to great wealth, it is the combination of these skills that will greatly amplify an individual's financial intelligence.

In summary

The Rich with Corporations	People Who Work for Corporations
1. Earn	1. Earn
2. Spend	2. Pay Taxes
3. Pay Taxes	3. Spend

As part of your overall financial strategy, we strongly recommend owning your own corporation wrapped around your assets.

THE RICH INVENT MONEY

The Rich Invent Money

*L*ast night, I took a break from writing and watched a TV program on the history of a young man named Alexander Graham Bell. Bell had just patented his telephone, and was having growing pains because the demand for his new invention was so strong. Needing a bigger company, he then went to the giant at that time, Western Union, and asked them if they would buy his patent and his tiny company. He wanted $100,000 for the whole package. The president of Western Union scoffed at him and turned him down, saying the price was ridiculous. The rest is history. A multi-billion-dollar industry emerged, and AT&T was born.

The evening news came on right after the story of Alexander Graham Bell ended. On the news was a story of another downsizing at a local company. The workers were angry and complained that the company ownership was unfair. A terminated manager of about 45 years of age had his wife and two babies at the plant and was begging the guards to let him talk to the owners to ask if they would reconsider his termination. He had just bought a house and was afraid of losing it. The camera focused in on his pleading for all the world to see. Needless to say, it held my attention.

I have been teaching professionally since 1984. It has been a great experience and rewarding. It is also a disturbing profession, for I have taught thousands of individuals and I see one thing in common in all of us, myself included. We all have tremendous potential, and we all are blessed with gifts. Yet, the one thing that holds all of us back is some degree of self-doubt. It is not so much the lack of technical information that holds us back, but more the lack of self-confidence. Some are more affected than others.

Once we leave school, most of us know that it is not as much a matter of college degrees or good grades that count. In the real world outside of academics, something more than just grades is required. I have heard it called "guts," "chutzpah," "balls," "audacity," "bravado," "cunning," "daring," "tenacity" and "brilliance." This factor, whatever it is labeled, ultimately decides one's future much more than school grades.

Inside each of us is one of these brave, brilliant and daring characters. There is also the flip side of that character: people who could get down on their knees and beg if necessary. After a year in Vietnam, as a Marine Corps pilot, I intimately got to know both of those characters inside of me. One is not better than the other.

Yet, as a teacher, I recognized that it was excessive fear and self-doubt that were the greatest detractors of personal genius. It broke my heart to see students know the answers, yet lack the courage to act on the answer. Often in the real world, it's not the smart that get ahead but the bold.

In my personal experience, your financial genius requires both technical knowledge as well as courage. If fear is too strong, the genius is suppressed. In my classes I strongly urge students to learn to take risks, to be bold, to let their genius convert that fear into power and brilliance. It works for some and just terrifies others. I have come to realize that for most people, when it comes to the subject of money, they would rather play it safe. I have had to field questions such as: Why take risks? Why should I bother developing my financial IQ? Why should I become financially literate?

And I answer, "Just to have more options."

There are huge changes up head. Just as I started with the story of the young inventor Alexander Graham Bell, in the coming years there will be more people just like him. There will be a hundred people like Bill Gates and hugely successful companies like Microsoft created every year, all over the world. And there also will be many more bankruptcies, layoffs and downsizing.

So why bother developing your financial IQ? No one can answer that but you. Yet, I can tell you why I myself do it. I do it because it is the most exciting time to be alive. I'd rather be welcoming change than dreading change. I'd rather be excited about making millions than worrying about not getting a raise. This period we are in now is a most exciting time, unprecedented in our world's history. Generations from now, people will look back at this period of time and remark at what an exciting era it must have been. It was the death of the old and birth of the new. It was full of turmoil and it was exciting.

So why bother developing your financial IQ? Because if you do, you will prosper greatly. And if you don't, this period of time will be a frightening one. It will be a time of watching people move boldly forward while others cling to decaying life rings.

Land was wealth 300 years ago. So the person who owned the land owned the wealth. Then, it was factories and production, and America rose to dominance. The industrialist owned the wealth. Today, it is information. And the person who has the most timely information owns the wealth. The problem is, information flies all around the world at the speed of light. The new wealth cannot be contained by boundaries and borders as land and factories were. The changes will be faster and more dramatic. There will be a dramatic increase in the number of new multimillionaires. There also will be those who are left behind.

Today, I find so many people struggling, often working harder, simply because they cling to old ideas. They want things to be the way they were; they resist change. I know people who are losing their jobs or their houses, and they blame technology or the economy or their boss. Sadly they fail to realize that they might be the problem. Old ideas are their biggest liability. It is a liability simply because they fail to realize that while that idea or way of doing something was an asset yesterday, yesterday is gone.

One afternoon I was teaching investing using a board game I had invented, CASHFLOW, as a teaching tool. A friend had brought someone along to attend the class. This friend of a friend was recently divorced, had been badly burned in the divorce settlement, and was now searching for some answers. Her friend thought the class might help.

The game was designed to help people learn how money works. In playing the game, they learn about the interaction of the income statement with the balance sheet. They learn how "cash flows" between the two and how the road to wealth is through striving to increase your monthly cash flow from the asset column to the point that it exceeds your monthly expenses. Once you accomplish this, you are able to get out of the "Rat Race" and out onto the "Fast Track".

As I have said, some people hate the game, some love it, and others miss the point. This woman missed a valuable opportunity to learn something. In the opening round, she drew a "doodad" card with the boat on it. At first she was happy. "Oh, I've got a boat." Then, as her friend tried to explain how the numbers worked on her income statement and balance sheet, she got frustrated because she had never liked math. The rest of her table waited while her friend continued explaining the relationship between the income statement, balance sheet and monthly cash flow. Suddenly, when she realized how the numbers worked, it dawned on her that her boat was eating her alive. Later on in the game, she was also "downsized" and had a child. It was a horrible game for her.

After the class, her friend came by and told me that she was upset. She had come to the class to learn about investing and did not like the idea that it took so long to play a silly game.

Her friend attempted to tell her to look within herself to see if the game "reflected" on herself in any way. With that suggestion, the woman demanded her money back. She said that the very idea that a game could be a reflection of her was ridiculous. Her money was promptly refunded and she left.

Since 1984, I have made millions simply by doing what the school system does not. In school, most teachers lecture. I hated lectures as a student; I was soon bored and my mind would drift.

In 1984, I began teaching via games and simulations. I always encouraged adult students to look at games as reflecting back to what they know, and what they needed to learn. Most importantly, a game reflects back on one's behavior. It's an instant feedback system. Instead of the teacher lecturing you, the game is feeding back a personalized lecture, custom made just for you.

The friend of the woman who left later called to give me an update. She said her friend was fine and had calmed down. In her cooling-off period, she could see some slight relationship between the game and her life.

Although she and her husband did not own a boat, they did own

112

everything else imaginable. She was angry after their divorce, both because he had run off with a younger woman and because after twenty years of marriage, they had accumulated little in the way of assets. There was virtually nothing for them to split. Their twenty years of married life had been incredible fun, but all they had accumulated was a ton of doodads.

She realized that her anger at doing the numbers—the income statement and balance sheet—came from her embarrassment of not understanding them. She had believed that finances were the man's job. She maintained the house and did the entertaining, and he handled the finances. She was now quite certain that in the last five years of their marriage, he had hidden money from her. She was angry at herself for not being more aware of where the money was going, as well as for not knowing about the other woman.

Just like a board game, the world is always providing us with instant feedback. We could learn a lot if we tuned in more. One day not long ago, I complained to my wife that the cleaners must have shrunk my pants. My wife gently smiled and poked me in the stomach to inform me that the pants had not shrunk, something else had expanded: me!

The game *CASHFLOW* was designed to give every player personal feedback. Its purpose is to give you options. If you draw the boat card and it puts you into debt, the question is, "Now what can you do?" How many different financial options can you come up with? That is the purpose of the game: to teach players to think and create new and various financial options.

I have watched this game played by more than 1,000 people. The people who get out of the "Rat Race" in the game the quickest are the people who understand numbers and have creative financial minds. They recognize different financial options. People who take the longest are people who are not familiar with numbers and often do not understand the power of investing. Rich people are often creative and take calculated risks.

There have been people playing *CASHFLOW* who gain lots of money in the game, but they don't know what to do with it. Most of them have not been financially successful in real life either. Everyone else seems to be getting ahead of them, even though they have money. And that is true in real life. There are a lot of people who have a lot of money and do not get ahead financially.

Limiting your options is the same as hanging on to old ideas. I have a friend from high school who now works at three jobs. Twenty years ago, he was the richest of all my classmates. When the local sugar plantation closed, the company he worked for went down with the plantation. In his mind, he had but one option, and that was the old option: work hard. The problem was, he couldn't find an equivalent job that recognized his seniority in the old company. As a result, he is overqualified for the jobs he currently has, so his salary is lower. He now works three jobs to earn enough to survive.

I have watched people playing *CASHFLOW* complaining that the "right" opportunity cards are not coming their way. So they sit there. I know people who do that in real life. They wait for the "right" opportunity.

I have watched people get the "right" opportunity card and then not have enough money. Then, they complain that they would have gotten out of the Rat Race if they had had more money. So they sit there. I know people in real life who do that also. They see all the great deals, but they have no money.

And I have people pull a great opportunity card, read it out loud and have no idea that it is a great opportunity. They have the money, the time is right, they have the card, but they can't see the opportunity staring at them. They fail to see how it fits into their financial plan for escaping the Rat Race. And I know more people like that than all the others combined. Most people have an opportunity of a lifetime flash right in front of them, and they fail to see it. A year later, they find out about it, after everyone else got rich.

Financial intelligence is simply having more options. If the opportunities aren't coming your way, what else can you do to improve your financial position? If an opportunity lands in your lap, and you have no money, and the bank won't talk to you, what else can you do to get the opportunity to work in your favor? If your hunch is wrong, and what you've been counting on doesn't happen, how can you turn a lemon into millions. That is financial intelligence. It is not so much what happens, but how many different financial solutions you can think of to turn a lemon into millions. It is how creative you are in solving financial problems.

Most people only know one solution: work hard, save and borrow. So why would you want to increase your financial intelligence?

Because you want to be the kind of person who creates your own luck. You take whatever happens and make it better. Few people realize that luck is created. Just as money is. And if you want to be luckier and create money instead of working hard, then your financial intelligence is important. If you are the kind of person who is waiting for the "right" thing to happen, you might wait for a long time. It's like waiting for all the traffic lights to be green for five miles before starting the trip.

As young boys, Mike and I were constantly told by my rich dad that "Money is not real." Rich dad occasionally reminded us of how close we came to the secret of money on that first day we got together and began "making money" out of plaster of paris. "The poor and middle class work for money," he would say. "The rich make money. The more real you think money is, the harder you will work for it. If you can grasp the idea that money is not real, you will grow richer faster."

"What is it?" was a question Mike and I often came back with. "What is money if it is not real?"

"What we agree it is," was all rich dad would say.

The single most powerful asset we all have is our mind. If it is trained well, it can create enormous wealth in what seems to be an instant. Wealth so far beyond the dreams of kings and queens 300 years ago. An untrained mind can also create extreme poverty that lasts lifetimes by teaching it to their families.

In the Information Age, money is increasing exponentially. A few individuals are getting ridiculously rich from nothing, just ideas and agreements. If you ask many people who trade stocks or other investments for a living, they see it done all the time. Often, millions can be made instantaneously from nothing. And by nothing, I mean no money was exchanged. It is done via agreement: a hand signal in a trading pit; a blip on a trader's screen in Lisbon from a trader's screen in Toronto, and back to Lisbon; a call to my broker to buy and a moment later to sell. Money did not change hands. Agreements did.

So why develop your financial genius? Only you can answer that. I can tell you why I have been developing this area of my intelligence. I do it because I want to make money fast. Not because I need to, but because I want to. It is a fascinating learning process. I develop my financial IQ because I want to participate in the fastest game and biggest game in the world. And in my own small way, I would like to be part of this unprecedented evolution of humanity, the era where humans work purely with their minds and not with their bodies. Besides, it is where the action is. It is what is happening. It's hip. It's scary. And it's fun.

That is why I invest in my financial intelligence, developing the most powerful asset I have. I want to be with people moving boldly forward. I do not want to be with those left behind.

I will give you a simple example of creating money. In the early 1990s the economy of Phoenix was horrible. I was watching the TV show "Good Morning America" when a financial planner came on and began forecasting doom and gloom. His advice was to "save money." Put $100 away every month, he said, and in 40 years you will be a multimillionaire."

Well, putting money away every month is a sound idea. It is one option—the option most people subscribe to. The problem is this: It blinds the person from what is really going on. They miss major opportunities for much more significant growth of their money. The world is passing them by.

As I said, the economy was terrible at that time. For investors, this is the perfect market condition. A chunk of my money was in the stock market and in apartment houses. I was short of cash. Because everyone was giving stuff away, I was buying. I was not saving money; I was investing. My wife and I had more than a million dollars in cash working in a market that was rising fast. It was the best opportunity to invest. The economy was terrible. I just could not pass up these small deals.

Houses that were once $100,000 were now $75,000. But instead of shopping at the local real estate office, I began shopping at the bankruptcy attorney's office, or the courthouse steps. In these shopping places, a $75,000 house could sometimes be bought for $20,000 or less. For $2,000, which was loaned to me from a friend for 90 days for $200, I gave an attorney a cashier's check as a down payment. While the acquisition was being processed, I ran an ad in the paper advertising a $75,000 house for only $60,000 and no money down. The phone rang hard and heavy. Prospective buyers were screened and once the property was legally mine, all the perspective buyers were allowed to look at the house. It was a feeding frenzy. The house sold in a few minutes. I asked for a $2,500 processing fee, which they gladly handed over, and the escrow and title company took over from there. I returned the $2,000 to my friend with an additional $200. He was happy, the home buyer was happy, the attorney was happy, and I was happy. I had sold a house for $60,000 that cost me $20,000. The $40,000 was created from money in my asset column in the form of a promissory note from the buyer. Total working time: five hours.

So now that you are financially literate and read numbers, I will show you why this is an example of money being invented.

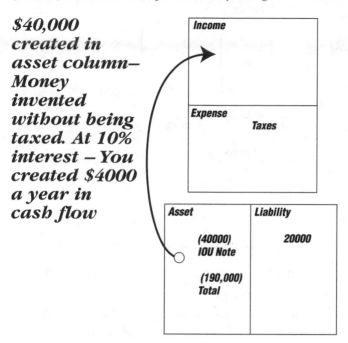

$40,000 created in asset column— Money invented without being taxed. At 10% interest – You created $4000 a year in cash flow

Income

Expense

Taxes

Asset

Liability

(40000) IOU Note

20000

(190,000) Total

During this depressed market, my wife and I were able to do six of these simple transactions in our spare time. While the bulk of our money was in larger properties and the stock market, we were able to create more than $190,000 in assets (notes at 10 percent interest) in those six buy, create and sell transactions. That comes to approximately $19,000 a year income, much of it sheltered through our private corporation. Much of that $19,000 a year goes to pay for our company cars, gas, trips, insurance, dinners with clients and other things. By the time the government gets a chance to tax that income, it's been spent on legally allowed pre-tax expenses.

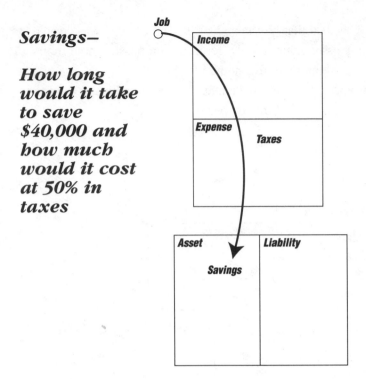

Savings—

How long would it take to save $40,000 and how much would it cost at 50% in taxes

Job

Income

Expense   Taxes

Asset   Liability

Savings

This was a simple example of how money is invented, created and protected using financial intelligence.

Ask yourself how long it would take to save $190,000. Would the bank pay you 10 percent interest on your money? And the note is good for 30 years. I hope they never pay me the $190,000. I have to pay a tax if they pay me the principle, and besides, $19,000 paid over 30 years is a little over $500,000 in income.

I have people ask what happens if the person doesn't pay. That does happen, and it's good news. The Phoenix real estate market, from 1994 to 1997, has been one of the hottest in the nation. That $60,000 home would be taken back and re-sold for $70,000, and another $2,500 is collected as a loan-processing fee. It would still be a zero-down transaction in the mind of the new buyer. And the process would go on.

So if you're quick, the first time I sold the house, I paid back the $2,000. Technically I have no money in the transaction. My return on investment (ROI) is infinity. It's an example of no money making a lot of money.

In the second transaction, when re-sold, I would have put $2,000 in my pocket and re-extended the loan to 30 years. What would my ROI be if I got paid money to make money? I do not know, but it sure beats saving $100 a month, which actually starts out as $150 because it's after-tax income for 40 years at 5 percent, and again you're taxed on the 5 percent. That is not too intelligent. It may be safe, but it's not smart.

Today, in 1997 as I write this book, the market conditions are exactly the opposite of five years ago. The real estate market of Phoenix is the envy of the U.S. Those houses we sold for $60,000 are now worth $110,000. There are foreclosure opportunities still available, but it will cost a valuable asset, my time, to go out looking for them. They are rare. But today, there are thousands of buyers looking for those deals, and only a few available that make financial sense. The market has changed. It is time to move on and look for other opportunities to put in the asset column.

"You can't do that here." "That is against the law." "You're lying."

I hear those comments much more often than "Can you show me how to do that?"

The math is simple. You do not need algebra or calculus. I don't write much because the escrow company handles the legal transaction and the servicing of the payments. I have no roofs to fix or toilets to unplug because the owners do that. It's their house. Occasionally someone does not pay. And that is wonderful because there are late fees, or they move out and the property is sold again. The court system handles that.

And it may not work in your area. The market conditions may be different. But the example illustrates how a simple financial process can create hundreds of thousands of dollars, with little money and low risk. It is an example of money being only an agreement. Anyone with a high school education can do it.

Yet, most people won't. Most people listen to the standard advice of "Work hard and save money."

For about 30 hours of work, approximately $190,000 was created in the asset column, and no taxes were paid.

Which one sounds harder to you?

1. Work hard, pay 50 percent in taxes, save what is left. Your savings then earns 5 percent, which is also taxed.
Or:
2. Take the time to develop your financial intelligence and harness the power of your brain and the asset column.

Add to that how much time it takes you, time being one of your greatest assets, to save $190,000 if you used option No. 1?

Now you may understand why I silently shake my head when I hear parents say, "My child is doing well in school and receiving a good education." It may be good, but is it adequate?

I know the above investment strategy is a small one. It is used to illustrate how small can grow into big. Again, my success reflects the importance of a strong financial foundation, which starts with strong financial education. I have said it before, yet it is worth repeating— financial intelligence is made up of these four main technical skills:

1. Financial literacy. The ability to read numbers.
2. Investment strategies. The science of money making money.
3. The market. Supply and demand. Alexander Graham Bell gave the market what it wanted. So did Bill Gates. A $75,000 house offered for $60,000 that cost $20,000 was also the result of seizing an opportunity created by the market. Somebody was buying, and someone was selling.
4. The law. The awareness of accounting, corporate, state and national rules and regulations. I recommend playing within the rules.

It is this basic foundation, or the combination of these skills, that is needed to be successful in the pursuit of wealth, whether it be through the buying of small homes, large apartments, companies, stocks, bonds, mutual funds, precious metals, baseball cards or the like.

By 1996, the real estate market had rebounded and everyone else was getting in. The stock market was booming, and everyone was getting in. The U.S. economy was getting back on its feet. I began selling in 1996 and was now traveling to Peru, Norway, Malaysia and the Philippines. The investments had changed. We were out of the real estate market, as far as buying goes. Now I just watch the values climb inside the asset column and will probably begin selling later this year. It depends on some law changes that may be passed in Congress. I suspect that some of those six little house deals will begin selling and the $40,000 note will be converted to cash. I need to call my accountant to be prepared for cash and seek ways to shelter it.

The point I would like to make is that investments come and go, the market goes up and goes down, economies improve and crash. The world is always handing you opportunities of a lifetime, every day of your life, but all too often we fail to see them. But they are there. And the more the world changes and the more technology changes, the more opportunities there will be to allow you and your family to be financially secure for generations to come.

So why bother developing your financial intelligence? Again, only you can answer that. I know why I continue to learn and develop. I do it because I know there are changes coming. I'd rather welcome change than cling to the past. I know there will be market booms and market crashes. I want to continually develop my financial intelligence because at each market change, some people will be on their knees begging for their jobs. Others, meanwhile, will take the lemons that life hands them—and we are all handed lemons occasionally—and turn them into millions. That's financial intelligence.

I am often asked about the lemons I have turned into millions. As a personal note, I hesitate using many more examples of personal investments. I hesitate because I am afraid it will come across as bragging or tooting my own horn. That is not my intention. I use the examples only as numerical and chronological illustrations of actual and simple cases. I use the examples because I want you to know that it is easy. It is easier, the more familiar you are with the four pillars of financial intelligence.

Personally, I use two main vehicles to achieve financial growth: real estate and small stocks. I use real estate as my foundation. Day in and day out, my properties provide cash flow and occasional spurts of growth in value. The small-cap stocks are used for fast growth.

I do not recommend anything that I do. The examples are just that, examples. If the opportunity is too complex and I do not understand the investment, I don't do it. Simple math and common sense is all that is needed to do well financially.

There are five reasons for using the examples.
1. To inspire people to learn more.
2. To let people know it is easy if the foundation is strong.
3. To show that anyone can achieve great wealth.
4. To show that there are millions of ways to achieve your goals.
5. To show that it's not rocket science.

In 1989, I used to jog through a lovely neighborhood in Portland, Oregon. It was a suburb that had little gingerbread houses. They were small and cute. I almost expected to see Little Red Riding Hood skipping down the sidewalk on her way to Granny's.

There were "for sale" signs everywhere. The timber market was terrible, the stock market had just crashed, and the economy was depressed. On one street, I noticed a for-sale sign that was up longer than most. It looked old. Jogging past it one day, I ran into the owner, who looked troubled.

"What are you asking for your house?" I asked.

The owner turned and smiled weakly. "Make me an offer," he said. "It's been for sale for over a year. Nobody even comes by anymore to look at it."

"I'll look," I said, and I bought the house a half hour later for $20,000 less than his asking price.

It was a cute little two-bedroom home, with gingerbread trim on all the windows. It was light blue with gray accents and had been built in 1930. Inside there was a beautiful rock fireplace, as well as two tiny bedrooms. It was a perfect rental house.

I gave the owner $5,000 down for a $45,000 house that was really worth $65,000, except that no one wanted to buy it. The owner moved out in a week, happy to be free, and my first tenant moved in, a local college professor. After the mortgage, expenses and management fees were paid, I put a little less than $40 in my pocket at the end of each month. Hardly exciting.

A year later, the depressed Oregon real estate market had begun to pick up. California investors, flush with money from their still-booming real estate market, were moving north and buying up Oregon and Washington.

I sold that little house for $95,000 to a young couple from California who thought it was a bargain. My capital gains of approximately $40,000 was placed into a 1031 tax-deferred exchange, and I went shopping for a place to put my money. In about a month, I found a 12-unit apartment house right next to the Intel plant in Beaverton, Oregon. The owners lived in Germany, had no idea what the place was worth, and again, just wanted to get out of it. I offered $275,000 for a $450,000 building. They agreed to $300,000. I bought it and held it for 2 years. Utilizing the same 1031 exchange process, we sold the building for $495,000 and bought a 30-unit apartment building in Phoenix, Arizona. We had moved to Phoenix by then to get out of the rain, and needed to sell anyway. Like the former Oregon market, the real estate market in Phoenix was depressed. The price of the 30-unit apartment building in Phoenix was $875,000, with $225,000 down. The cash flow from the 30 units was a little over $5,000 a month. The Arizona market began moving up and, in 1996, a Colorado investor offered us $1.2 million for the property.

My wife and I considered selling, but we decided to wait to see if the capital-gains law will be changed by Congress. If it does change, we suspect the property will go up another 15 to 20 percent. Besides, the $5,000 a month provides a nice cash flow.

The point of this example is how a small amount can grow into a large amount. Again, it is a matter of understanding financial statements, investment strategies, a sense of the market and the laws. If people are not versed in these subjects, then obviously they must follow standard dogma, which is to play it safe, diversify and only invest in secure investments. The problem with "secure" investments is that they are often sanitized. That is, made so safe that the gains are less.

Most large brokerage houses will not touch speculative transactions to protect themselves and their clients. And that is a wise policy.

The really hot deals are not offered to people who are novices. Often, the best deals that make the rich even richer are reserved for those who understand the game. It is technically illegal to offer someone who is considered not "sophisticated" such speculative deals, but, of course, it happens.

The more so-called "sophisticated" I get, the more opportunities come my way. Another case for developing your financial intelligence, over a lifetime, is simply that more opportunities are presented to you. And the greater your financial intelligence, the easier it is to tell whether a deal is good. It's your intelligence that can spot a bad deal, or make a bad deal good. The more I learn—and there is a lot to learn—the more money I make simply because I gain experience and wisdom as the years go on. I have friends who are playing it safe, working hard at their profession, and failing to gain financial wisdom, which does take time to develop.

My overall philosophy is to plant seeds inside my asset column. That is my formula. I start small and plant seeds. Some grow; some don't.

Inside our real estate corporation, we have several million dollars' worth of property. It is our own REIT, or real estate investment trust.

The point I'm making is that most of those millions started out as little $5,000 to $10,000 investments. All of those down payments were fortunate to catch a fast-rising market, increase tax free, trading in and out several times over a number of years.

We also own a stock portfolio, surrounded by a corporation that my wife and I call our personal mutual fund. We have friends who deal specifically with investors like us that have extra money each month to invest. We buy high-risk, speculative private companies that are just about to go public on a stock exchange in the United States or Canada. An example of how fast gains can be made are 100,000 shares purchased for 25 cents each before the company goes public. Six months later, the company is listed, and the 100,000 shares now are worth $2 each. If the company is well-managed, the price keeps going up, and the stock may go to $20 or more per share. There are years when our $25,000 has gone to a million in less than a year.

It is not gambling if you know what you're doing. It is gambling if you're just throwing money into a deal and praying. The idea in anything is to use your technical knowledge, wisdom and love of the game to cut the odds down, to lower the risk. Of course, there is always risk. It is financial intelligence that improves the odds. Thus, what is risky for one person is less risky to someone else. That is the primary reason I constantly encourage people to invest more in their financial education than in the stock, real estate or other markets. The smarter you are, the better chance you have of beating the odds.

The stock plays I personally invest in are extremely high risk for most people and absolutely not recommended. I have been playing that game since 1979 and have paid more than my share in dues. But if you will reread why investments such as these are high risk for most people, you may be able to set your life up differently, so that the ability to take $25,000 and turn it into $1 million in a year is low risk for you.

As stated earlier, nothing I have written is a recommendation. It is only used as an example of what is simple and possible. What I do is small potatoes in the scheme of things, yet for the average individual, a passive income of more than $100,000 a year is nice and not hard to achieve. Depending on the market and how smart you are, it could be done in five to ten years. If you keep your living expenses modest, $100,000 coming in as additional income is pleasant, regardless of whether you work. You can work if you like or take time off if you choose and use the government tax system in your favor, rather than against you.

My personal basis is real estate. I love real estate because it's stable and slow moving. I keep the base solid. The cash flow is fairly steady and, if properly managed, has a good chance of increasing in value. The beauty of a solid base of real estate is that it allows me to be somewhat riskier with the more speculative stocks I buy.

If I make great profits in the stock market, I pay my capital-gains tax on the gain and then reinvest what's left in real estate, again further securing my asset foundation.

A last word on real estate. I have traveled all over the world and taught investing. In every city, I hear people say you cannot buy real estate cheap. That is not my experience. Even in New York or Tokyo, or just on the outskirts of the city, are prime bargains overlooked by most people. In Singapore, currently undergoing high real estate prices, there are still bargains to be found within a short driving distance. So whenever I hear someone say, "You can't do that here," pointing at me, I remind them that maybe the real statement is, "I don't know how to do that here. . .yet."

Great opportunities are not seen with your eyes. They are seen with your mind. Most people never get wealthy simply because they are not trained financially to recognize opportunities right in front of them.

I am often asked, "How do I start?"

In the last chapter, I offer ten steps that I followed on the road to my financial freedom. But always remember to have fun. This is only a game. Sometimes you win and sometimes you learn. But have fun. Most people never win because they're more afraid of losing. That is why I found school so silly. In school we learn that mistakes are bad, and we are punished for making them. Yet, if you look at the way humans are designed to learn, we learn by making mistakes. We learn to walk by falling down. If we never fell down, we would never walk. The same is true for learning to ride a bike. I still have scars on my knees, but today I can ride a bike without thinking. The same is true for getting rich. Unfortunately the main reason most people are not rich is because they are terrified of losing. Winners are not afraid of losing. But losers are. Failure is part of the process of success. People who avoid failure also avoid success.

I look at money much like my game of tennis. I play hard, make mistakes, correct, make more mistakes, correct and get better. If I lose the game, I reach across the net, shake my opponent's hand, smile and say, "See you next Saturday."

There are two kinds of investors.

1. The first and most common type are people who buy a packaged investment. They call a retail outlet, such as a real estate company or a stockbroker or a financial planner, and they buy something. It could be a mutual fund, a REIT, a stock or a bond. It is a good clean and simple way of investing. An example would be a shopper who goes to a computer store and buys a computer right off the shelf.

2. The second type are investors who create investments. This investor usually assembles a deal, much like there are people who buy components of computers and put it together. It's like customizing. I do not know the first thing about putting components of a computer together. But I do know how to put pieces of opportunities together, or know people who do.

It is this second type of investor that is most probably the professional investor. Sometimes it may take years for all the pieces to come together. And sometimes they never do come together. It was this second type of investor my rich dad encouraged me to be. It is important to learn how to put the pieces together because that is where the huge wins are, and sometimes some huge losses if the tide goes against you.

If you want to be the second type of investor, you need to develop three main skills. These skills are in addition to those required to become financially intelligent:

1. How to find an opportunity that everyone else has missed. You see with your mind what others miss with their eyes. For example, a friend bought this rundown old house. It was spooky to look at. Everyone wondered why he bought it. What he saw that we did not was that the house came with four extra empty lots. He realized that by going to the title company. After buying the house, he tore it down and sold the five lots to a builder for three times what he paid for the entire package. He made $75,000 for two months' work. It's not a lot of money, but it sure beats minimum wage, and it's not technically difficult.

2. How to raise money. The average person only goes to the bank. This second type of investor needs to know how to raise capital, and there

are many ways that don't require a bank. To get started, I learned how to buy houses without a bank. It was not so much the houses, but the learned skill of raising money that is priceless.

All too often I hear people say, "The bank won't lend me money." Or "I don't have the money to buy it." If you want to be a Type 2 investor, you need to learn how to do that which stops most people. In other words, a majority of people let their lack of money stop them from making a deal. If you can avoid that obstacle, you will be millions ahead of those who don't learn those skills. There have been many times I have bought a house, a stock or an apartment building without a penny in the bank. I once bought an apartment house for $1.2 million. I did what is called "Tying it up," with a written contract between seller and buyer. I then raised the $100,000 deposit, which bought me 90 days to raise the rest of the money. Why did I do it? Simply because I knew it was worth $2 million. I never raised the money. Instead, the person who put up the $100,000 gave me $50,000 for finding the deal, he took over my position, and I walked away. Total working time: three days. Again, it's what you know more than what you buy. Investing is not buying. It's more a case of knowing.

3. How to organize smart people. Intelligent people are those who work with or hire a person who is more intelligent than they are. When you need advice, make sure you choose your advisor wisely.

There is a lot to learn, but the rewards can be astronomical. If you do not want to learn those skills, then being a Type 1 investor is highly recommended. It is what you know that is your greatest wealth. It is what you do not know that is your greatest risk.

There is always risk, so learn to manage risk instead of avoid it.

WORK TO LEARN – DON'T WORK FOR MONEY

Work to Learn —
Don't Work
for Money

*I*n 1995, I granted an interview with a newspaper in Singapore. The young female reporter was on time, and the interview got under way immediately. We sat in the lobby of a luxurious hotel, sipping coffee and discussing the purpose of my visit to Singapore. I was to share the platform with Zig Ziglar. He was speaking on motivation, and I was speaking on "The Secrets of the Rich."

"Someday, I would like to be a best-selling author like you," she said. I had seen some of the articles she had written for the paper, and I was impressed. She had a tough, clear style of writing. Her articles held a reader's interest.

"You have a great style," I said in reply. "What holds you back from achieving your dream?"

"My work does not seem to go anywhere," she said quietly. "Everyone says that my novels are excellent, but nothing happens. So I keep my job with the paper. At least it pays the bills. Do you have any suggestions?"

"Yes, I do," I said brightly. "A friend of mine here in Singapore runs a school that trains people to sell. He runs sales-training courses for many of the top corporations here in Singapore, and I think attending one of his courses would greatly enhance your career."

She stiffened. "Are you saying I should go to school to learn to sell?" I nodded.

"You aren't serious, are you?"

Again, I nodded. "What is wrong with that?" I was now backpeddling. She was offended by something, and now I was wishing I had not said anything. In my attempt to be helpful, I found myself defending my suggestion.

"I have a master's degree in English Literature. Why would I go to school to learn to be a salesperson? I am a professional. I went to school to be trained in a profession so I would not have to be a salesperson. I hate salespeople. All they want is money. So tell me why I should study sales?" She was now packing her briefcase forcibly. The interview was over.

On the coffee table sat a copy of an earlier best-selling book I wrote. I picked it up as well as the notes she had jotted down on her legal pad. "Do you see this?" I said pointing to her notes.

She looked down at her notes. "What," she said, confused.

Again, I pointed deliberately to her notes. On her pad she had written "Robert Kiyosaki, best-selling author."

"It says 'best-selling author,' not best 'writing' author."

Her eyes widened immediately.

"I am a terrible writer. You are a great writer. I went to sales school. You have a master's degree. Put them together and you get a 'best-selling author' and a 'best-writing author.' "

Anger flared from her eyes. "I'll never stoop so low as to learn how to sell. People like you have no business writing. I am a professionally trained writer and you are a salesman. It is not fair."

The rest of her notes were put away, and she hurried out through the large glass doors into the humid Singapore morning.

At least she gave me a fair and favorable write-up the next morning.

The world is filled with smart, talented, educated and gifted people. We meet them every day. They are all around us.

A few days ago, my car was not running well. I pulled into a garage, and the young mechanic had it fixed in just a few minutes. He knew what was wrong by simply listening to the engine. I was amazed.

The sad truth is, great talent is not enough.

I am constantly shocked at how little talented people earn. I heard the other day that less than 5 percent of Americans earn more than $100,000 a year. I have met brilliant, highly educated people who earn less than $20,000 a year. A business consultant who specializes in the medical trade was telling me how many doctors, dentists and chiropractors struggle financially. All this time, I thought that when they graduated, the dollars would pour in. It was this business consultant who gave me the phrase, "They are one skill away from great wealth."

What this phrase means is that most people need only to learn and master one more skill and their income would jump exponentially. I have mentioned before that financial intelligence is a synergy of accounting, investing, marketing and law. Combine those four technical skills and making money with money is easier. When it comes to money, the only skill most people know is to work hard.

The classic example of a synergy of skills was that young writer for the newspaper. If she diligently learned the skills of sales and marketing, her income would jump dramatically. If I were her, I would take some courses in advertising copywriting as well as sales. Then, instead of working at the newspaper, I would seek a job at an advertising agency. Even if it were a cut in pay, she would learn how to communicate in "short cuts" that are used in successful advertising. She also would spend time learning public relations, an important skill. She would learn how to get millions in free publicity. Then, at night and on weekends, she could be writing her great novel. When it was finished, she would be better able to sell her book. Then, in a short while, she could be a "best-selling author."

When I first came out with my first book *If You Want To Be Rich and Happy, Don't Go to School?* a publisher suggested I change the title to The Economics of Education. I told the publisher that with a title like that, I would sell two books: one to my family and one to my best friend. The problem is, they would expect it for free. The obnoxious title *If You Want To Be Rich and Happy, Don't Go to School?* was chosen because we knew it would get tons of publicity. I am pro-education and believe in education reform. Otherwise, why would I continue to press for changing our antiquated educational system? So I chose a title that would get me on more TV and radio shows, simply because I was willing to be controversial. Many people thought I was a fruitcake, but the book sold and sold.

When I graduated from the U.S. Merchant Marine Academy in 1969, my educated dad was happy. Standard Oil of California had hired me for its oil-tanker fleet. I was a third mate, and the pay was low compared with my classmates, but it was OK for a first real job after college. My starting pay was about $42,000 a year, including overtime, and I only had to work for seven months. I had five months of vacation. If I had wanted to, I could have taken the run to Vietnam with a subsidiary shipping company, and easily doubled my pay instead of taking the five months' vacation.

I had a great career ahead of me, yet I resigned after six months with the company and joined the Marine Corps to learn how to fly. My educated dad was devastated. Rich dad congratulated me.

In school and in the workplace, the popular opinion is the idea of "specialization." That is, in order to make more money or get promoted, you need to "specialize." That is why medical doctors immediately begin to seek a specialty such as orthopedics or pediatrics. The same is true for accountants, architects, lawyers, pilots and others.

My educated dad believed in the same dogma. That is why he was thrilled when he eventually achieved his doctorate. He often admitted that schools reward people who study more and more about less and less.

Rich dad encouraged me to do exactly the opposite. "You want to know a little about a lot" was his suggestion. That is why for years I worked in different areas of his companies. For awhile, I worked in his accounting department. Although I would probably never have been an accountant, he wanted me to learn via "osmosis." Rich dad knew I would pick up "jargon" and a sense of what is important and what is not. I also worked as a bus boy and construction worker, as well as in sales, reservations and marketing. He was "grooming" Mike and me. That is why he insisted we sit in on the meetings with his bankers, lawyers, accountants and brokers. He wanted us to know a little about every aspect of his empire.

When I quit my high-paying job with Standard Oil, my educated dad had a heart-to-heart with me. He was bewildered. He could not understand my decision to resign from a career that offered high pay, great benefits, lots of time off, and opportunity for promotion. When he asked me one evening, "Why did you quit?" I could not explain it to him, as much as I tried. My logic did not fit his logic. The big problem was that my logic was my rich dad's logic.

Job security meant everything to my educated dad. Learning meant everything to my rich dad.

Educated dad thought I went to school to learn to be a ship's officer. Rich dad knew that I went to school to study international trade. So as a student, I made cargo runs, navigating large freighters, oil tankers and passenger ships to the Far East and the South Pacific. Rich dad emphasized that I stay in the Pacific instead of taking ships to Europe because he knew that the "emerging nations" were in Asia, not Europe. While most of my classmates, including Mike, were partying at their fraternity houses, I was studying trade, people, business styles and cultures in Japan, Taiwan, Thailand, Singapore, Hong Kong, Vietnam, Korea, Tahiti, Samoa and the Philippines. I also was partying, but it was not in any frat house. I grew up rapidly.

Educated dad just could not understand why I decided to quit and join the Marine Corps. I told him I wanted to learn to fly, but really I wanted to learn to lead troops. Rich dad explained to me that the hardest part of running a company is managing people. He had spent three years in the Army; my educated dad was draft-exempt. Rich dad told me of the value of learning to lead men into dangerous situations. "Leadership is what you need to learn next," he said. "If you're not a good leader, you'll get shot in the back, just like they do in business."

Returning from Vietnam in 1973, I resigned my commission, even though I loved flying. I found a job with Xerox Corp. I joined it for one reason, and it was not for the benefits. I was a shy person, and the thought of selling was the most frightening subject in the world. Xerox has one of the best sales-training programs in America.

Rich dad was proud of me. My educated dad was ashamed. Being an intellectual, he thought that salespeople were below him. I worked with Xerox for four years until I overcame my fear of knocking on doors and being rejected. Once I could consistently be in the top five in sales, I again resigned and moved on, leaving behind another great career with an excellent company.

In 1977, I formed my first company. Rich dad had groomed Mike and me to take over companies. So I now had to learn to form them and put them together. My first product, the nylon and velcro wallet, was manufactured in the Far East and shipped to a warehouse in New York, near where I had gone to school. My formal education was complete, and it was time to test my wings. If I failed, I went broke. Rich dad thought it best to go broke before 30. "You still have time to recover" was his advice. On the eve of my 30th birthday, my first shipment left Korea for New York.

Today, I still do business internationally. And as my rich dad encouraged me to do, I keep seeking the emerging nations. Today my investment company invests in South America, Asia, Norway and Russia.

There is an old cliche that goes, "Job is an acronym for 'Just Over Broke.'" And unfortunately, I would say that the saying applies to millions of people. Because school does not think financial intelligence is an intelligence, most workers "live within their means." They work and they pay the bills.

There is another horrible management theory that goes, "Workers work hard enough to not be fired, and owners pay just enough so that workers won't quit." And if you look at the pay scales of most companies, again I would say there is a degree of truth in that statement.

The net result is that most workers never get ahead. They do what they've been taught to do: "Get a secure job." Most workers focus on working for pay and benefits that reward them in the short term, but is often disastrous in the long run.

Instead I recommend to young people to seek work for what they will learn, more than what they will earn. Look down the road at what skills they want to acquire before choosing a specific profession and before getting trapped in the "Rat Race."

Once people are trapped in the lifelong process of bill paying, they become like those little hamsters running around in those little metal wheels. Their little furry legs are spinning furiously, the wheel is turning furiously, but come tomorrow morning, they'll still be in the same cage: great job.

In the movie *Jerry Maguire*, starring Tom Cruise, there are many great one liners. Probably the most memorable is "Show me the money." But there is one line I thought most truthful. It comes from the scene where Tom Cruise is leaving the firm. He has just been fired, and he is asking the entire company "Who wants to come with me?" And the whole place is silent and frozen. Only one woman speaks up and says, "I'd like to but I'm due for a promotion in three months."

That statement is probably the most truthful statement in the whole movie. It is the type of statement that people use to keep themselves busy working away to pay bills. I know my educated dad looked forward to his pay raise every year, and every year he was disappointed. So he would go back to school to earn more qualifications so he could get another raise, but again, it would be another disappointment.

The question I often ask people is, "Where is this daily activity taking you?" Just like the little hamster, I wonder if people look at where their hard work is taking them. What does the future hold?

Cyril Brickfield, the former executive director of The American Association of Retired People, reports that "private pensions are in a state of chaos. First of all, 50 percent of the workforce today has no pension. That alone should be of great concern. And 75 to 80 percent of the other 50 percent have ineffective pensions that pay $55 or $150 or $300 a month."

In his book *The Retirement Myth*, Craig S. Karpel writes: "I visited the headquarters of a major national pension consulting firm and met with a managing director who specializes in designing lush retirement plans for top management. When I asked her what people who don't have corner offices will be able to expect in the way of pension income, she said with a confident smile: 'The Silver Bullet.'

" 'What,' I asked, 'is The Silver Bullet?'

"She shrugged, 'If baby boomers discover they don't have enough money to live on when they're older, they can always blow their brains out.' " Karpel goes on to explain the difference between the old Defined Benefit retirement plans and the new 401K plans which are riskier. It is not a pretty picture for most people working today. And that is just for retirement. When medical fees and long-term nursing home care are added to the picture, the picture is frightening. In his 1995 book, he indicates that nursing-home fees run from $30,000 to $125,000 per year. He went to a clean no-frills nursing home in his area and found the price to be $88,000 a year in 1995.

Already, many hospitals in countries with socialized medicine need to make tough decisions such as "Who will live and who will die?" They make those decisions purely on how much money they have and how old the patients are. If the patient is old, they often will give the medical care to someone younger. The older poor patient gets put to the back of the line. So just as the rich can afford better education, the rich will be able to keep themselves alive, while those who have little wealth will die.

So I wonder, are workers looking into the future or just until their next paycheck, never questioning where they are headed?

When I speak to adults who want to earn more money, I always recommend the same thing. I suggest taking a long view of their life. Instead of simply working for the money and security, which I admit are important, I suggest they take a second job that will teach them a second skill. Often I recommend joining a network marketing company, also called multilevel marketing, if they want to learn sales skills. Some of these companies have excellent training programs that help people get over their fear of failure and rejection, which are the main reasons people are unsuccessful. Education is more valuable than money, in the long run.

When I offer this suggestion, I often hear in response, "Oh that is too much hassle," or "I only want to do what I am interested in."

To the statement of "It's too much of a hassle," I ask, "So you would rather work all your life giving 50 percent of what you earn to the government?" To the other statement—"I only do what I am interested in"—I say, "I'm not interested in going to the gym, but I go because I want to feel better and live longer."

Unfortunately, there is some truth to the old statement "You can't teach an old dog new tricks." Unless a person is used to changing, it's hard to change.

But for those of you who might be on the fence when it comes to the idea of working to learn something new, I offer this word of encouragement: Life is much like going to the gym. The most painful part is deciding to go. Once you get past that, it's easy. There have been many days I have dreaded going to the gym, but once I am there and in motion, it is a pleasure. After the workout is over, I am always glad I talked myself into going.

If you are unwilling to work to learn something new and insist on, instead, becoming highly specialized within your field, make sure the company you work for is unionized. Labor unions are designed to protect specialists.

My educated dad, after falling from grace with the governor, became the head of the teachers union in Hawaii. He told me that it was the hardest job he ever held. My rich dad, on the other hand, spent his life doing his best to keep his companies from becoming unionized. He was successful. Although the unions came close, rich dad was always able to fight them off.

Personally, I take no sides because I can see the need for and the benefits of both sides. If you do as school recommends, become highly specialized, then seek union protection. For example, had I continued on with my flying career, I would have sought a company that had a strong pilots union. Why? Because my life would be dedicated to learn a skill that was valuable in only one industry. If I were pushed out of that industry, my life's skills would not be as valuable to another industry. A displaced senior pilot—with 100,000 hours of heavy airline transport time, earning $150,000 a year—would have a hard time finding an equivalent high-paying job in school teaching. The skills do not necessarily transfer from industry to industry, because the skills the pilots are paid for in the airline industry are not as important in, say, the school system.

The same is true even for doctors today. With all the changes in medicine, many medical specialists are needing to conform to medical organizations such as HMO's. Schoolteachers definitely need to be union members. Today in America, the teachers union is the largest and the richest labor union of all. The NEA, National Education Association, has tremendous political clout. Teachers need the protection of their union because their skills are also of limited value to an industry outside of education. So the rule of thumb is, "Highly specialized, then unionize." It's the smart thing to do.

When I ask the classes I teach, "How many of you can cook a better hamburger than McDonald's?" almost all the students raise their hands. I then ask, "So if most of you can cook a better hamburger, how come McDonald's makes more money than you?"

The answer is obvious: McDonald's is excellent at business systems. The reason so many talented people are poor is because they focus on building a better hamburger and know little to nothing about business systems.

A friend of mine in Hawaii is a great artist. He makes a sizable amount of money. One day his mother's attorney called to tell him that she had left him $35,000. That is what was left of her estate after the attorney and the government took their shares. Immediately, he saw an opportunity to increase his business by using some of this money to advertise. Two months later, his first four-color, full-page ad appeared in an expensive magazine that targeted the very rich. The ad ran for three months. He received no replies from the ad, and all of his inheritance is now gone. He now wants to sue the magazine for misrepresentation.

This is a common case of someone who can build a beautiful hamburger, but knows little about business. When I asked him what he learned, his only reply was that "advertising salespeople are crooks." I then asked him if he would be willing to take a course in sales and a course in direct marketing. His reply, "I don't have the time, and I don't want to waste my money."

The world is filled with talented poor people. All too often, they're poor or struggle financially or earn less than they are capable of, not because of what they know but because of what they do not know. They focus on perfecting their skills at building a better hamburger rather than the skills of selling and delivering the hamburger. Maybe McDonald's does not make the best hamburger, but they are the best at selling and delivering a basic average burger.

Poor dad wanted me to specialize. That was his view on how to be paid more. Even after being told by the governor of Hawaii that he could no longer work in state government, my educated dad continued to encourage me to get specialized. Educated dad then took up the cause of the teachers union, campaigning for further protection and benefits for these highly skilled and educated professionals. We argued often, but I know he never agreed that overspecialization is what caused the need for union protection. He never understood that the more specialized you become, the more you are trapped and dependent on that specialty.

Rich dad advised that Mike and I "groom" ourselves. Many corporations do the same thing. They find a young bright student out of business school and begin "grooming" that person to someday take over the company. So these bright young employees do not specialize in one department; they are moved from department to department to learn all the aspects of business systems. The rich often "groom" their children or the children of others. By doing so, their children gain an overall knowledge of the operations of the business and how the various departments interrelate.

For the World War II generation, it was considered "bad" to skip from company to company. Today, it is considered smart. Since people will skip from company to company, rather than seek greater specialization, why not seek to "learn" more than "earn." In the short term, it may earn you less. In the long term, it will pay off in large dividends.

The main management skills needed for success are:

1. The management of cash flow.
2. The management of systems (including yourself and time with family).
3. The management of people.

The most important specialized skills are sales and understanding marketing. It is the ability to sell—therefore, to communicate to another human being, be it a customer, employee, boss, spouse or child—that is the base skill of personal success. It is communication skills such as writing, speaking and negotiating that are crucial to a life of success. It is a skill that I work on constantly, attending courses or buying educational tapes to expand my knowledge.

As I have mentioned, my educated dad worked harder and harder the more competent he became. He also became more trapped the more specialized he got. Although his salary went up, his choices diminished. Soon after he was locked out of government work, he found out how vulnerable he really was professionally. It is like professional athletes who suddenly are injured or are too old to play. Their once high-paying position is gone, and they have limited skills to fall back on. I think that is why my educated dad sided so much with unions after that. He realized how much a union would have benefited him.

Rich dad encouraged Mike and me to know a little about a lot. He encouraged us to work with people smarter than we were and to bring smart people together to work as a team. Today it would be called a synergy of professional specialities.

Today, I meet ex-schoolteachers earning hundreds of thousands of dollars a year. They earn that much because they have specialized skills in their field as well as other skills. They can teach as well as sell and market. I know of no other skills to be more important than selling as well as marketing. The skills of selling and marketing are difficult for most people primarily due to their fear of rejection. The better you are at communicating, negotiating and handling your fear of rejection, the easier life is. Just as I advised that newspaper writer who wanted to become a "best-selling author," I advise anyone else today. Being technically specialized has its strengths as well as its weaknesses. I have friends who are geniuses, but they cannot communicate effectively with other human beings and, as a result, their earnings are pitiful. I advise them to just spend a year learning to sell. Even if they earn nothing, their communication skills will improve. And that is priceless.

In addition to being good learners, sellers and marketers, we need to be good teachers as well as good students. To be truly rich, we need to be able to give as well as to receive. In cases of financial or professional struggle, there is often a lack of giving and receiving. I know many people who are poor because they are neither good students nor good teachers.

Both of my dads were generous men. Both made it a practice to give first. Teaching was one of their ways of giving. The more they gave, the more they received. One glaring difference was in the giving of money. My rich dad gave lots of money away. He gave to his church, to charities, to his foundation. He knew that to receive money, you had to give money. Giving money is the secret to most great wealthy families. That is why there are organizations like the Rockefeller Foundation and the Ford Foundation. These are organizations designed to take their wealth and increase it, as well as give it away in perpetuity.

My educated dad always said, "When I have some extra money, I'll give it." The problem was, there was never any extra. So he worked harder to draw more money in rather than focus on the most important law of money: "Give and you shall receive." Instead, he believed in "Receive and then you give."

In conclusion, I became both dads. One part of me is a hard-core capitalist who loves the game of money making money. The other side is a socially responsible teacher who is deeply concerned with this ever-widening gap between the haves and have nots. I personally hold the archaic educational system primarily responsible for this growing gap.

BEGINNINGS

CHAPTER EIGHT

Overcoming Obstacles

*O*nce people have studied and become financially literate, they may still face roadblocks to becoming financially independent. There are five main reasons why financially literate people may still not develop abundant asset columns. Asset columns that could produce large sums of cash flow. Asset columns that could free them to live the life they dream of, instead of working full time just to pay bills. The five reasons are:

1. Fear.
2. Cynicism.
3. Laziness.
4. Bad habits.
5. Arrogance.

Reason No. 1. Overcoming the fear of losing money. I have never met anyone who really likes losing money. And in all my years, I have never met a rich person who has never lost money. But I have met a lot of poor people who have never lost a dime. . .investing, that is.

The fear of losing money is real. Everyone has it. Even the rich. But it's not fear that is the problem. It's how you handle fear. It's how you handle losing. It's how you handle failure that makes the difference in one's life. That goes for anything in life, not just money. The primary difference between a rich person and a poor person is how they handle that fear.

It's OK to be fearful. It's OK to be a coward when it comes to money. You can still be rich. We're all heroes at something and cowards at something else. My friend's wife is an emergency room nurse. When she sees blood, she flies into action. When I mention investing, she runs away. When I see blood, I don't run. I pass out.

My rich dad understood phobias about money. "Some people are terrified of snakes. Some people are terrified about losing money. Both are phobias," he would say. So his solution to the phobia of losing money was this little rhyme:

"If you hate risk and worry. . .start early."

That's why banks recommend savings as a habit when you're young. If you start young, it's easy to be rich. I won't go into it here, but there is a large difference between a person who starts saving at age 20 versus age 30. A staggering difference.

It is said that one of the wonders of the world is the power of compound interest. The purchase of Manhattan Island is said to be one of the greatest bargains of all time. New York was purchased for $24 in trinkets and beads. Yet, if that $24 had been invested, at 8 percent annually, that $24 would have been worth more than $28 trillion by 1995. Manhattan could be repurchased with money left over to buy much of L.A., especially at 1995's real estate prices.

My neighbor works for a major computer company. He has been there 25 years. In five more years he will leave the company with $4 million in his 401k retirement plan. It is invested mostly in high-growth mutual funds, which he will convert to bonds and government securities. He'll only be 55 when he gets out, and he will have a passive cash flow of over $300,000 a year, more than he makes from his salary. So it can be done, even if you hate losing or hate risk. But you must start early and definitely set up a retirement plan, and you should hire a financial planner you trust to guide you before investing in anything.

But what if you don't have much time left or would like to retire early? How do you handle the fear of losing money?

My poor dad did nothing. He simply avoided the issue, refusing to discuss the subject.

My rich dad, on the other hand, recommended that I think like a Texan. "I like Texas and Texans," he used to say. "In Texas, everything is bigger. When Texans win, they win big. And when they lose, it's spectacular."

"They like losing?" I asked.

"That's not what I'm saying. Nobody likes losing. Show me a happy loser, and I'll show you a loser," said rich dad. "It's a Texan's attitude toward risk, reward and failure I'm talking about. It's how they handle life. They live it big. Not like most of the people around here, living like roaches when it comes to money. Roaches terrified that someone will shine a light on them. Whimpering when the grocery clerk shortchanges them a quarter."

Rich dad went on to explain.

"What I like best is the Texas attitude. They're proud when they win, and they brag when they lose. Texans have a saying, "If you're going to go broke, go big. You don't want to admit you went broke over a duplex. Most people around here are so afraid of losing, they don't have a duplex to go broke with."

He constantly told Mike and me that the greatest reason for lack of financial success was because most people played it too safe. "People are so afraid of losing that they lose" were his words.

Fran Tarkenton, a one-time great NFL quarterback, says it still another way: "Winning means being unafraid to lose."

In my own life, I've noticed that winning usually follows losing. Before I finally learned to ride a bike, I first fell down many times. I've never met a golfer who has never lost a golf ball. I've never met people who have fallen in love who have never had their heart broken. And I've never met someone rich who has never lost money.

So for most people, the reason they don't win financially is because the pain of losing money is far greater than the joy of being rich. Another saying in Texas is, "Everyone wants to go to Heaven, but no one wants to die." Most people dream of being rich, but are terrified of losing money. So they never get to Heaven.

Rich dad used to tell Mike and me stories about his trips to Texas. "If you really want to learn the attitude of how to handle risk, losing and failure, go to San Antonio and visit the Alamo. The Alamo is a great story of brave people who chose to fight, knowing there was no hope of success against overwhelming odds. They chose to die instead of surrendering. It's an inspiring story worthy of study; nonetheless, it's still a tragic military defeat. They got their butts kicked. A failure if you will. They lost. So how do Texans handle failure? They still shout, 'Remember the Alamo!' "

Mike and I heard this story a lot. He always told us this story when he was about to go into a big deal and he was nervous. After he had done all his due diligence and now it was put up or shut up, he told us this story. Every time he was afraid of making a mistake, or losing money, he told us this story. It gave him strength, for it reminded him that he could always turn a financial loss into a financial win. Rich dad knew that failure would only make him stronger and smarter. It's not that he wanted to lose; he just knew who he was and how he would take a loss. He would take a loss and make it a win. That's what made him a winner and others losers. It gave him the courage to cross the line when others backed out. "That's why I like Texans so much. They took a great failure and turned it into a tourist destination that makes them millions."

But probably his words that mean the most to me today are these: "Texans don't bury their failures. They get inspired by them. They take their failures and turn them into rallying cries. Failure inspires Texans to become winners. But that formula is not just the formula for Texans. It is the formula for all winners."

Just as I also said that falling off my bike was part of learning to ride. I remember falling off only made me more determined to learn to ride. Not less. I also said that I have never met a golfer who has never lost a ball. To be a top professional golfer, losing a ball or a tournament only inspires golfers to be better, to practice harder, to study more. That's what makes them better. For winners, losing inspires them. For losers, losing defeats them.

Quoting John D. Rockefeller, "I always tried to turn every disaster into an opportunity."

And being Japanese-American, I can say this. Many people say that Pearl Harbor was an American mistake. I say it was a Japanese mistake. From the movie *Tora, Tora, Tora*, a somber Japanese admiral says to his cheering subordinates, "I am afraid we have awakened a sleeping giant." "Remember Pearl Harbor" became a rallying cry. It turned one of America's greatest losses into the reason to win. This great defeat gave America strength, and America soon emerged as a world power.

Failure inspires winners. And failure defeats losers. It is the biggest secret of winners. It's the secret that losers do not know. The greatest secret of winners is that failure inspires winning; thus, they're not afraid of losing. Repeating Fran Tarkenton's quote, "Winning means being unafraid to lose." People like Fran Tarkenton are not afraid of losing because they know who they are. They hate losing, so they know that losing will only inspire them to become better. There is a big difference between hating losing and being afraid to lose. Most people are so afraid of losing money that they lose. They go broke over a duplex. Financially they play life too safe and too small. They buy big houses and big cars, but not big investments. The main reason that over 90 percent of the American public struggles financially is because they play not to lose. They don't play to win.

They go to their financial planners or accountants or stockbrokers and buy a balanced portfolio. Most have lots of cash in CDs, low-yield bonds, mutual funds that can be traded within a mutual-fund family, and a few individual stocks. It is a safe and sensible portfolio. But it is not a winning portfolio. It is a portfolio of someone playing not to lose.

Don't get me wrong. It's probably a better portfolio than more than 70 percent of the population, and that's frightening. Because a safe portfolio is a lot better than no portfolio. It's a great portfolio for someone who loves safety. But playing it safe and going "balanced" on your investment portfolio is not the way successful investors play the game. If you have little money and you want to be rich, you must first be "focused," not "balanced." If you look at anyone successful, at the start they were not balanced. Balanced people go nowhere. They stay in one spot. To make progress, you must first go unbalanced. Just look at how you make progress walking.

Thomas Edison was not balanced. He was focused. Bill Gates was not balanced. He was focused. Donald Trump is focused. George Soros is focused. George Patton did not take his tanks wide. He focused them and blew through the weak spots in the German line. The French went wide with the Maginot Line, and you know what happened to them.

If you have any desire of being rich, you must focus. Put a lot of your eggs in a few baskets. Do not do what poor and middle class people do: put their few eggs in many baskets.

If you hate losing, play it safe. If losing makes you weak, play it safe. Go with balanced investments. If you're over 25 years old and are terrified of taking risks, don't change. Play it safe, but start early. Start accumulating your nest egg early because it will take time.

But if you have dreams of freedom—of getting out of the rat race— the first question to ask yourself is, "How do I respond to failure?" If failure inspires you to win, maybe you should go for it—but only maybe. If failure makes you weak or causes you to throw temper tantrums—like spoiled brats who call an attorney to file a lawsuit every time something does not go their way—then play it safe. Keep your daytime job. Or buy bonds or mutual funds. But remember, there is risk in those financial instruments also, even though they are safer.

I say all this, mentioning Texas and Fran Tarkenton, because stacking the asset column is easy. It's really a low-aptitude game. It doesn't take much education. Fifth-grade math will do. But staking the asset column is a high-attitude game. It takes guts, patience and a great attitude toward failure. Losers avoid failing. And failure turns losers into winners. Just remember the Alamo.

Reason No. 2. Overcoming cynicism. "The sky is falling. The sky is falling." Most of us know the story of "Chicken Little," who ran around warning the barnyard of impending doom. We all know people who are that way. But we all have a "Chicken Little" inside each of us.

And as I stated earlier, the cynic is really a little chicken. We all get a little chicken when fear and doubt cloud our thoughts.

All of us have doubts. "I'm not smart." "I'm not good enough." "So and so is better than me." Or our doubts often paralyze us. We play the "What if?" game. "What if the economy crashes right after I invest?" Or "What if I lose control and I can't pay the money back?" "What if things don't go as I planned?" Or we have friends or loved ones who will remind us of our shortcomings regardless of whether we ask. They often say, "What makes you think you can do that?" Or "If it's such a good idea, how come someone else hasn't done it?" Or "That will never work. You don't know what you're talking about." These words of doubt often get so loud that we fail to act. A horrible feeling builds in our stomach. Sometimes we can't sleep. We fail to move forward. So we stay with what is safe and opportunities pass us by. We watch life passing by as we sit immobilized with a cold knot in our body. We have all felt this at one time in our lives, some more than others.

Peter Lynch of Fidelity Magellan mutual fund fame refers to warnings about the sky falling as "noise," and we all hear it.

"Noise" is either created inside our heads or comes from outside. Often from friends, family, co-workers and the media. Lynch recalls the time during the 1950s when the threat of nuclear war was so prevalent in the news that people began building fallout shelters and storing food and water. If they had invested that money wisely in the market, instead of building a fallout shelter, they'd probably be financially independent today.

When the riots broke out in Los Angeles a few years ago, gun sales went up all over the country. A person dies from rare hamburger meat in Washington State and the Arizona Health Department orders restaurants to have all beef cooked well-done. A drug company runs a national TV commercial showing people catching the flu. The ad runs in February. Colds go up as well as sales of their cold medicine.

Most people are poor because when it comes to investing, the world is filled with Chicken Littles running around yelling, "The sky is falling. The sky is falling." And Chicken Littles are effective because everyone of us is a little chicken. It often takes great courage to not let rumors and talk of doom and gloom affect your doubts and fears.

In 1992, a friend named Richard came from Boston to visit my wife and me in Phoenix. He was impressed with what we had done through stocks and real estate. The prices of real estate in Phoenix were depressed. We spent two days with him showing him what we thought were excellent opportunities for cash flow and capital appreciation.

My wife and I are not real estate agents. We are strictly investors. After identifying a unit in a resort community, we called an agent who sold it to him that afternoon. The price was a mere $42,000 for a two-bedroom townhome. Similar units were going for $65,000. He had found a bargain. Excited, he bought it and returned to Boston.

Two weeks later, the agent called to say that our friend had backed out. I called immediately to find out why. All he said was that he talked to his neighbor, and his neighbor told him it was a bad deal. He was paying too much.

I asked Richard if his neighbor was an investor. Richard said "no." When I asked why he listened to him, Richard got defensive and simply said he wanted to keep looking.

The real estate market in Phoenix turned, and by 1994, that little unit was renting for $1,000 a month—$2,500 in the peak winter months. The unit was worth $95,000 in 1995. All Richard had to put down was $5,000 and he would have had a start at getting out of the rat race. Today, he still has done nothing. And the bargains in Phoenix are still here; you just have to look a lot harder.

Richard's backing out did not surprise me. It's called "buyer's remorse," and it affects all of us. It's those doubts that get us. The little chicken won, and a chance at freedom was lost.

In another example, I hold a small portion of my assets in tax lien certificates instead of CDs. I earn 16 percent per year on my money, which certainly beats the 5 percent the bank offers. The certificates are secured by real estate and enforced by state law, which is also better than most banks. The formula they're bought on makes them safe. They just lack liquidity. So I look at them as 2 to 7-year CDs. Almost every time I tell someone, especially if they have money in CDs, that I hold my money this way, they will tell me it's risky. They tell me why I should not do it. When I ask them where they get their information, they say from a friend or an investment magazine. They've never done it, and they're telling someone who's doing it why they shouldn't. The lowest yield I look for is 16 percent, but people who are filled with doubt are willing to accept 5 percent. Doubt is expensive.

My point is that it's those doubts and cynicism that keep most people poor and playing it safe. The real world is simply waiting for you to get rich. Only a person's doubts keep them poor. As I said, getting out of the rat race is technically easy. It doesn't take much education, but those doubts are cripplers for most people.

"Cynics never win," said rich dad. "Unchecked doubt and fear creates a cynic. Cynics criticize, and winners analyze" was another of his favorite sayings. Rich dad explained that criticism blinded while analysis opened eyes. Analysis allowed winners to see that critics were blind, and to see opportunities that everyone else missed. And finding what people miss is key to any success.

Real estate is a powerful investment tool for anyone seeking financial independence or freedom. It is a unique investment tool. Yet, every time I mention real estate as a vehicle, I often hear, "I don't want to fix toilets." That's what Peter Lynch calls "noise." That's what my rich dad would say is the cynic talking. Someone who criticizes and does not analyze. Someone who lets their doubts and fears close their mind instead of open their eyes.

So when someone says, "I don't want to fix toilets," I want to fire back, "What makes you think I want to?" They're saying a toilet is more important than what they want. I talk about freedom from the rat race, and they focus on toilets. That is the thought pattern that keeps most people poor. They criticize instead of analyze.

" 'I don't wants' hold the key to your success," rich dad would say.

Because I, too, do not want to fix toilets, I shop hard for a property manager who does fix toilets. And by finding a great property manager who runs houses or apartments, well, my cash flow goes up. But more importantly a great property manager allows me to buy a lot more real estate since I don't have to fix toilets. A great property manager is key to success in real estate. Finding a good manager is more important to me than the real estate. A great property manager often hears of great deals before real estate agents do, which makes them even more valuable.

That is what rich dad meant by " 'I don't wants' hold the key to your success." Because I do not want to fix toilets either, I figured out how to buy more real estate and expedite my getting out of the rat race. The people who continue to say "I don't want to fix toilets" often deny themselves the use of this powerful investment vehicle. Toilets are more important than their freedom.

In the stock market, I often hear people say, "I don't want to lose money." Well, what makes them think I or anyone else likes losing money? They don't make money because they chose to not lose money. Instead of analyzing, they close their minds to another powerful investment vehicle, the stock market.

In December 1996, I was riding with a friend past our neighborhood gas station. He looked up and saw that the price of oil was going up. My friend is a worry wart or a "Chicken Little." To him, the sky is always going to fall, and it usually does, on him.

When we got home, he showed me all the stats as to why the price of oil was going to go up over the next few years. Statistics I had never seen before, even though I already owned a substantial share block of an existing oil company. With that information, I immediately began looking for and found a new undervalued oil company that was about to find some oil deposits. My broker was excited about this new company, and I bought 15,000 shares for 65 cents per share.

In February 1997, this same friend and I drove by the same gas station, and sure enough, the price per gallon had gone up nearly 15 percent. Again, the "Chicken Little" worried and complained. I smiled because in January 1997, that little oil company hit oil and those 15,000 shares went up to more than $3 per share since he had first given me the tip. And the price of gas will continue to go up if what my friend says is true.

Instead of analyzing, their little chicken closes their mind. If most people understood how a "stop" worked in stock-market investing, there would be more people investing to win instead of investing not to lose. A "stop" is simply a computer command that sells your stock automatically if the price begins to drop, helping to minimize your losses and maximize some gains. It's a great tool for those who are terrified of losing.

So whenever I hear people focusing on their "I don't wants," rather than what they do want, I know the "noise" in their head must be loud. Chicken Little has taken over their brain and is yelling, "The sky is falling and toilets are breaking." So they avoid their "don't wants," but they pay a huge price. They may never get what they want in life.

Rich dad gave me a way of looking at Chicken Little. "Just do what Colonel Sanders did." At the age of 66, he lost his business and began to live on his Social Security check. It wasn't enough. He went around the country selling his recipe for fried chicken. He was turned down 1,009 times before someone said "yes." And he went on to become a multimillionaire at an age when most people are quitting. "He was a brave and tenacious man," rich dad said of Harlan Sanders.

So when you're in doubt and feeling a little afraid, just do what Col. Sanders did to his little chicken. He fried it.

Reason No. 3. Laziness. Busy people are often the most lazy. We have all heard stories of a businessman who works hard to earn money. He works hard to be a good provider for his wife and children. He spends long hours at the office and brings work home on weekends. One day he comes home to an empty house. His wife has left with the kids. He knew he and his wife had problems, but rather than work to make the relationship strong, he stayed busy at work. Dismayed, his performance at work slips and he loses his job.

Today, I often meet people who are too busy to take care of their wealth. And there are people too busy to take care of their health. The cause is the same. They're busy, and they stay busy as a way of avoiding something they do not want to face. Nobody has to tell them. Deep down they know. In fact, if you remind them, they often respond with anger or irritation.

If they aren't busy at work or with the kids, they're often busy watching TV, fishing, playing golf or shopping. Yet, deep down they know they are avoiding something important. That's the most common form of laziness. Laziness by staying busy.

So what is the cure for laziness? The answer is a little greed.

For many of us, we were raised thinking of greed or desire as bad. "Greedy people are bad people," my mom use to say. Yet, we all have inside of us this yearning to have nice things, new things or exciting things. So to keep that emotion of desire under control, often parents found ways of suppressing that desire with guilt.

"You only think about yourself. Don't you know you have brothers and sisters?" was one of my mom's favorites. Or "You want me to buy you what?" was a favorite of my dad. "Do you think we're made of money? Do you think money grows on trees? We're not rich people, you know."

It wasn't so much the words but the angry guilt-trip that went with the words that got to me.

Or the reverse guilt-trip was the "I'm sacrificing my life to buy this for you. I'm buying this for you because I never had this advantage when I was a kid." I have a neighbor who is stone broke, but can't park his car in his garage. The garage is filled with toys for his kids. Those spoiled brats get everything they ask for. "I don't want them to know the feeling of want" are his everyday words. He has nothing set aside for their college or his retirement, but his kids have every toy ever made. He recently got a new credit card in the mail and took his kids to visit Las Vegas. "I'm doing it for the kids," he said with great sacrifice.

Rich dad forbade the words "I can't afford it."

In my real home, that's all I heard. Instead, rich dad required his children to say, "How can I afford it?" His reasoning, the words "I can't afford it" shut down your brain. It didn't have to think anymore. "How can I afford it?" opened up the brain. Forced it to think and search for answers.

But most importantly, he felt the words "I can't afford it" were a lie. And the human spirit knew it. "The human spirit is very, very, powerful," he would say. "It knows it can do anything." By having a lazy mind that says, "I can't afford it," a war breaks out inside you. Your spirit is angry, and your lazy mind must defend its lie. The spirit is screaming, "Come on. Let's go to the gym and work out." And the lazy mind says, "But I'm tired. I worked really hard today." Or the human spirit says, "I'm sick and tired of being poor. Let's get out there and get rich." To which the lazy mind says, "Rich people are greedy. Besides it's too much bother.

It's not safe. I might lose money. I'm working hard enough as it is. I've got too much to do at work anyway. Look at what I have to do tonight. My boss wants it finished by the morning."

"I can't afford it" also brings up sadness. A helplessness that leads to despondency and often depression. "Apathy" is another word. "How can I afford it?" opens up possibilities, excitement and dreams. So rich dad was not so concerned about what you wanted to buy, but that "How can I afford it?" created a stronger mind and a dynamic spirit.

Thus, he rarely gave Mike or me anything. Instead he would ask, "How can you afford it?" and that included college, which we paid for ourselves. It was not the goal but the process of attaining the goal we desired that he wanted us to learn.

The problem I sense today is that there are millions of people who feel guilty about their greed. It's an old conditioning from their childhood. Their desire to have the finer things that life offers. Most have been conditioned subconsciously to say, "You can't have that," or "You'll never afford that."

When I decided to exit the rat race, it was simply a question. "How can I afford to never work again?" And my mind began to kick out answers and solutions. The hardest part was fighting my real parents' dogma of "We can't afford that." Or "Stop thinking only about yourself." Or "Why don't you think about others?" and other such words designed to instill guilt to suppress my greed.

So how do you beat laziness? The answer is a little greed. It's that radio station WII-FM, which stands for "What's In It-For Me?" A person needs to sit down and ask, "What's in it for me if I'm healthy, sexy and good looking?" Or "What would my life be like if I never had to work again?" Or "What would I do if I had all the money I needed?" Without that little greed, the desire to have something better, progress is not made. Our world progresses because we all desire a better life. New inventions are made because we desire something better. We go to school and study hard because we want something better. So whenever you find yourself avoiding something you know you should be doing, then the only thing to ask yourself is "What's in it for me?" Be a little greedy. It's the best cure for laziness.

Too much greed, however, as anything in excess can be, is not good. But just remember what Michael Douglas said in the movie *Wall Street*. "Greed is good." Rich dad said it differently: "Guilt is worse than greed.

For guilt robs the body of its soul." And to me, Eleanor Roosevelt said it best: "Do what you feel in your heart to be right—for you'll be criticized anyway. You'll be damned if you do, and damned if you don't."

Reason No. 4. Habits. Our lives are a reflection of our habits more than our education. After seeing the movie *Conan*, starring Arnold Schwarzenegger, a friend said, "I'd love to have a body like Schwarzenegger." Most of the guys nodded in agreement.

"I even heard he was really puny and skinny at one time," another friend added.

"Yeah, I heard that too," another one added. "I heard he has a habit of working out almost every day in the gym."

"Yeah, I'll bet he has to."

"Nah," said the group cynic. "I'll bet he was born that way. Besides, let's stop talking about Arnold and get some beers."

This is an example of habits controlling behavior. I remember asking my rich dad about the habits of the rich. Instead of answering me outright, he wanted me to learn through example, as usual.

"When does your dad pay his bills?" rich dad asked.

"The first of the month," I said.

"Does he have anything left over?" he asked.

"Very little," I said.

"That's the main reason he struggles," said rich dad. "He has bad habits."

"Your dad pays everyone else first. He pays himself last, but only if he has anything left over."

"Which he usually doesn't," I said. "But he has to pay his bills, doesn't he? You're saying he shouldn't pay his bills?"

"Of course not," said rich dad. "I firmly believe in paying my bills on time. I just pay myself first. Before I pay even the government."

"But what happens if you don't have enough money?" I asked. "What do you do then?"

"The same," said rich dad. "I still pay myself first. Even if I'm short of money. My asset column is far more important to me than the government."

"But," I said. "Don't they come after you?"

"Yes, if you don't pay," said rich dad. "Look, I did not say not to pay. I just said I pay myself first, even if I'm short of money."

"But," I replied. "How do you do that?"

159

"It's not how. The question is 'Why,' " rich dad said.

"OK, why?"

"Motivation," said rich dad "Who do you think will complain louder if I don't pay them—me or my creditors?"

"Your creditors will definitely scream louder than you," I said, responding to the obvious. "You wouldn't say anything if you didn't pay yourself."

"So you see, after paying myself, the pressure to pay my taxes and the other creditors is so great that it forces me to seek other forms of income. The pressure to pay becomes my motivation. I've worked extra jobs, started other companies, traded in the stock market, anything just to make sure those guys don't start yelling at me. That pressure made me work harder, forced me to think, and all in all made me smarter and more active when it comes to money. If I had paid myself last, I would have felt no pressure, but I'd be broke."

"So it is the fear of the government or other people you owe money to that motivates you?"

"That's right," said rich dad. "You see, government bill collectors are big bullies. So are bill collectors in general. Most people give into these bullies. They pay them and never pay themselves. You know the story of the 96-pound weakling who gets sand kicked in his face?"

I nodded. "I see that ad for weightlifting and bodybuilding lessons in the comic books all the time."

"Well, most people let the bullies kick sand in their faces. I decided to use the fear of the bully to make me stronger. Others get weaker. Forcing myself to think about how to make extra money is like going to the gym and working out with weights. The more I work my mental money muscles out, the stronger I get. Now, I'm not afraid of those bullies.

I liked what rich dad was saying. "So if I pay myself first, I get financially stronger, mentally and fiscally."

Rich dad nodded.

"And if I pay myself last, or not at all, I get weaker. So people like bosses, managers, tax collectors, bill collectors and landlords push me around all my life. Just because I don't have good money habits."

Rich dad nodded. "Just like the 96-pound weakling."

Reason No. 5. Arrogance. Arrogance is ego plus ignorance.

"What I know makes me money. What I don't know loses me

160

money. Every time I have been arrogant, I have lost money. Because when I'm arrogant, I truly believe that what I don't know is not important," rich dad would often tell me.

I have found that many people use arrogance to try to hide their own ignorance. It often happens when I am discussing financial statements with accountants or even other investors.

They try to bluster their way through the discussion. It is clear to me that they don't know what they're talking about. They're not lying, but they are not telling the truth.

There are many people in the world of money, finances and investments who have absolutely no idea what they're talking about. Most people in the money industry are just spouting off sales pitches like used-car salesmen.

When you know you are ignorant in a subject, start educating yourself by finding an expert in the field or find a book on the subject.

GETTING STARTED

CHAPTER NINE

Getting Started

I wish I could say acquiring wealth was easy for me, but it wasn't.

So in response to the question "How do I start?" I offer the thought process I go through on a day-by-day basis. It really is easy to find great deals. I promise you that. It's just like riding a bike. After a little wobbling, it's a piece of cake. But when it comes to money, it's the determination to get through the wobbling that's a personal thing.

To find million-dollar "deals of a lifetime" requires us to call on our financial genius. I believe that each of us has a financial genius within us. The problem is, our financial genius lies asleep, waiting to be called upon. It lies asleep because our culture has educated us into believing that the love of money is the root of all evil. It has encouraged us to learn a profession so we can work for money, but failed to teach us how to have money work for us. It taught us not to worry about our financial future, our company or the government would take care of us when our working days are over. However, it is our children, educated in the same school system, who will end up paying for it. The message is still to work hard, earn money and spend it, and when we run short, we can always borrow more.

Unfortunately, 90 percent of the Western world subscribes to the above dogma, simply because it's easier to find a job and work for money. If you are not one of the masses, I offer you the following ten steps to awaken your financial genius. I simply offer you the steps I have personally followed. If you want to follow some of them, great. If you don't, make up your own. Your financial genius is smart enough to develop its own list.

While in Peru, with a gold miner of 45 years, I asked him how he was so confident about finding a gold mine. He replied, "There is gold everywhere. Most people are not trained to see it."

And I would say that is true. In real estate, I can go out and in a day come up with four or five great potential deals, while the average person will go out and find nothing. Even looking in the same neighborhood. The reason is they have not taken the time to develop their financial genius.

I offer you the following ten steps as a process to develop your God-given powers. Powers only you have control over.

1. I NEED A REASON GREATER THAN REALITY: The power of spirit. If you ask most people if they would like to be rich or financially free, they would say "yes." But then reality sets in. The road seems too long with too many hills to climb. It's easier to just work for money and hand the excess over to your broker.

I once met a young woman who had dreams of swimming for the U.S Olympic team. The reality was, she had to get up every morning at 4 a.m. to swim for three hours before going to school. She did not party with her friends on Saturday night. She had to study and keep her grades up, just like everyone else.

When I asked her what compelled her with such super-human ambition and sacrifice, she simply said, "I do it for myself and the people I love. It's love that gets me over the hurdles and sacrifices."

A reason or a purpose is a combination of "wants" and "don't wants." When people ask me what my reason for wanting to be rich is, it is a combination of deep emotional "wants" and "don't wants."

I will list a few. First the "don't wants," for they create the "wants." I don't want to work all my life. I don't want what my parents aspired for, which was job security and a house in the suburbs. I don't like being an employee. I hated that my dad always missed my football games because he was so busy working on his career. I hated it when my dad worked hard all his life and the government took most of what he worked for at his death. He could not even pass on what he worked so hard for when he died. The rich don't do that. They work hard and pass it on to their children.

Now the wants. I want to be free to travel the world and live in the lifestyle I love. I want to be young when I do this. I want to simply be free. I want control over my time and my life. I want money to work for me.

Those are my deep-seated, emotional reasons. What are yours? If they are not strong enough, then the reality of the road ahead may be greater than your reasons. I have lost money and been set back many times, but it was the deep emotional reasons that kept me standing up and going forward. I wanted to be free by age 40, but it took me until I was 47 with many learning experiences along the way.

As I said, I wish I could say it was easy. It wasn't, but it wasn't hard either. But without a strong reason or purpose, anything in life is hard.

IF YOU DO NOT HAVE A STRONG REASON, THERE IS NO SENSE READING FURTHER. IT WILL SOUND LIKE TOO MUCH WORK.

2. I CHOOSE DAILY: The power of choice. That is the main reason people want to live in a free country. We want the power to choose.

Financially, with every dollar we get in our hands, we hold the power to choose our future to be rich, poor or middle class. Our spending habits reflect who we are. Poor people simply have poor spending habits.

The benefit I had as a boy was that I loved playing Monopoly constantly. Nobody told me Monopoly was only for kids, so I just kept playing the game as an adult. I also had a rich dad who pointed out to me the difference between an asset and a liability. So a long time ago, as a little boy, I chose to be rich, and I knew that all I had to do was learn to acquire assets, real assets. My best friend, Mike, had an asset column handed to him, but he still had to choose to learn to keep it. Many rich families lose their assets in the next generation simply because there was no one trained to be a good steward over their assets.

Most people choose not to be rich. For 90 percent of the population, being rich is "too much of a hassle." So they invent sayings that go, "I'm not interested in money." Or "I'll never be rich." Or "I don't have to worry, I'm still young." Or "When I make some money, then I'll think about my future." Or "My husband/wife handles the finances." The problem with those statements is they rob the person who chooses to think such thoughts of two things: one is time, which is your most precious asset, and two is learning. Just because you have no money, it should not be an excuse to not learn. But that is a choice we all make daily, the choice of what we do with our time, our money and what we put in our heads. That is the power of choice. All of us have choice. I just choose to be rich, and I make that choice every day.

INVEST FIRST IN EDUCATION: In reality, the only real asset you have is your mind, the most powerful tool we have dominion over. Just as I said about the power of choice, each of us has the choice of what we put in our brain once we're old enough. You can watch MTV all day, or read golf magazines, or go to ceramics class or a class on financial planning. You choose. Most people simply buy investments rather than first invest in learning about investing.

A friend of mine, who is a rich woman, recently had her apartment burglarized. The thieves took her TV and VCR and left all the books she reads. And we all have that choice. Again, 90 percent of the population buys TV sets and only about 10 percent buy books on business or tapes on investments.

So what do I do? I go to seminars. I like it when they are at least two days long because I like to immerse myself in a subject. In 1973, I was watching TV and this guy came on advertising a three-day seminar on how to buy real estate for nothing down. I spent $385 and that course has made me at least $2 million, if not more. But more importantly, it bought me life. I don't have to work for the rest of my life because of that one course. I go to at least two such courses every year.

I love audio tapes. The reason: I can rewind quickly. I was listening to a tape by Peter Lynch, and he said something I completely disagreed with. Instead of becoming arrogant and critical, I simply pushed "rewind" and I listened to that five-minute stretch of tape at least twenty times. Possibly more. But suddenly, by keeping my mind open, I understood why he said what he said. It was like magic. I felt like I had a window into the mind of one of the greatest investors of our time. I gained tremendous depth and insight into the vast resources of his education and experience.

The net result: I still have the old way I used to think, and I have Peter's way of looking at the same problem or situation. I have two thoughts instead of one. One more way to analyze a problem or trend, and that is priceless. Today, I often say, "How would Peter Lynch do this, or Donald Trump or Warren Buffett or George Soros?" The only way I can access their vast mental power is to be humble enough to read or listen to what they have to say. Arrogant or critical people are often people with low self-esteem who are afraid of taking risks. You see, if you learn something new, you are then required to make mistakes in order to fully understand what you have learned.

If you have read this far, arrogance is not one of your problems. Arrogant people rarely read or buy tapes. Why should they? They are the center of the universe.

There are so many "intelligent" people who argue or defend when a new idea clashes with the way they think. In this case, their so-called "intelligence" combined with "arrogance" equals "ignorance". Each of us knows people who are highly educated, or believe they are smart, but their balance sheet paints a different picture. A truly intelligent person welcomes new ideas, for new ideas can add to the synergy of other accumulated ideas. Listening is more important than talking. If that was not true, God would not have given us two ears and only one mouth. Too many people think with their mouth instead of listening to absorb new ideas and possibilities. They argue instead of asking questions.

I take a long view on my wealth. I do not subscribe to the "Get rich quick" mentality most lottery players or casino gamblers have. I may go in and out of stocks, but I am long on education. If you want to fly an airplane, I advise taking lessons first. I am always shocked at people who buy stocks or real estate, but never invest in their greatest asset, their mind. Just because you bought a house or two does not make you an expert at real estate.

3. **CHOOSE FRIENDS CAREFULLY:** The power of association. First of all, I do not choose my friends by their financial statements. I have friends who have actually taken the vow of poverty as well as friends who earn millions every year. The point is I learn from all of them, and I consciously make the effort to learn from them.

Now I will admit that there are people I have actually sought out because they had money. But I was not after their money; I was seeking their knowledge. In some cases, these people who had money have become dear friends, but not all.

But there is one distinction that I would like to point out. I've noticed that my friends with money talk about money. And I do not mean brag. They're interested in the subject. So I learn from them, and they learn from me. My friends, whom I know are in dire straits financially, do not like talking about money, business or investing. They often think it rude or unintellectual. So I also learn from my friends who struggle financially. I find out what not to do.

I have several friends who have generated over a billion dollars in their short lifetimes. The three of them report the same phenomenon: Their friends who have no money have never come to them to ask them how they did it. But they do come asking for one of two things, or both: 1. a loan, or 2. a job.

A WARNING: Don't listen to poor or frightened people. I have such friends, and I love them dearly, but they are the "Chicken Littles" of life. When it comes to money, especially investments, "The sky is always falling." They can always tell you why something won't work. The problem is, people listen to them, but people who blindly accept doom-and-gloom information are also "Chicken Littles." As that old saying goes, "Chickens of a feather agree together."

If you watch CNBC, which is a goldmine of investment information, they often have a panel of so-called "experts." One expert will say the market is going to crash, and the other will say it's going to boom. If you're smart, you listen to both. Keep your mind open because both have valid points. Unfortunately, most poor people listen to "Chicken Little."

I have had more close friends try to talk me out of a deal or an investment. A few years ago, a friend told me he was excited because he found a 6 percent certificate of deposit. I told him I earn 16 percent from the state government. The next day he sent me an article about why my investment was dangerous. I have received 16 percent for years now, and he still receives 6 percent.

I would say that one of the hardest things about wealth building is to be true to yourself and be willing to not go along with the crowd. For in the market, it is usually the crowd that shows up late and is slaughtered. If a great deal is on the front page, it's too late in most instances. Look for a new deal. As we used to say as surfers: "There is always another wave." People who hurry and catch a wave late usually are the ones who wipe out.

Smart investors don't time markets. If they miss a wave, they search for the next one and get themselves in position. Why this is hard for most investors is because buying what is not popular is frightening to them. Timid investors are like sheep going along with the crowd. Or their greed gets them in when wise investors have already taken their profits and moved on. Wise investors buy an investment when it's not popular. They know their profits are made when they buy, not when they sell. They wait patiently. As I said, they do not time the market. Just like a surfer, they get in position for the next big swell.

It's all "insider trading." There are forms of insider trading that are illegal, and there are forms of insider trading that are legal. But either way, it's insider trading. The only distinction is how far away from the inside are you? The reason you want to have rich friends who are close to the inside is because that is where the money is made. It's made on information. You want to hear about the next boom, get in and get out before the next bust. I'm not saying do it illegally, but the sooner you know, the better your chances are for profits with minimal risk. That is what friends are for. And that is financial intelligence.

4. **MASTER A FORMULA AND THEN LEARN A NEW ONE:** The power of learning quickly. In order to make bread, every baker follows a recipe, even if it's only held in their head. The same is true for making money. That's why money is often called "dough."

Most of us have heard the saying "You are what you eat." I have a different slant on the same saying. I say, "You become what you study." In other words, be careful what you study and learn, because your mind is so powerful that you become what you put in your head. For example, if you study cooking, you then tend to cook. You become a cook. If you don't want to be a cook anymore, then you need to study something else. Let's say, a schoolteacher. After studying teaching, you often become a teacher. And so on. Choose what you study carefully.

When it comes to money, the masses generally have one basic formula they learned in school. And that is, work for money. The formula I see that is predominant in the world is that every day millions of people get up and go to work, earn money, pay bills, balance checkbooks, buy some mutual funds and go back to work. That is the basic formula, or recipe.

If you're tired of what you're doing, or you're not making enough, it's simply a case of changing the formula via which you make money.

Years ago, when I was 26, I took a weekend class called "How to Buy Real Estate Foreclosures." I learned a formula. The next trick was to have the discipline to actually put into action what I had learned. That is where most people stop. For three years, while working for Xerox, I spent my spare time learning to master the art of buying foreclosures. I've made several million dollars using that formula, but today, it's too slow and too many other people are doing it.

So after I mastered that formula, I went in search of other formulas. For many of the classes, I did not use the information I learned directly, but I always learned something new.

I have attended classes designed for only derivative traders, also a class for commodity option traders and a class for Chaologists. I was way out of my league, being in a room full of people with doctorates in nuclear physics and space science. Yet, I learned a lot that made my stock and real estate investing more meaningful and lucrative.

Most junior colleges and community colleges have classes on financial planning and buying of traditional investments. They are great places to start.

So I always search for a faster formula. That is why, on a fairly regular basis, I make more in a day than many people will make in their lifetime.

Another side note. In today's fast-changing world, it's not so much what you know anymore that counts, because often what you know is old. It is how fast you learn. That skill is priceless. It's priceless in finding faster formulas—recipes, if you will, for making dough. Working hard for money is an old formula born in the day of cave men.

5. **PAY YOURSELF FIRST:** The power of self-discipline. If you cannot get control of yourself, do not try to get rich. You might first want to join the Marine Corps or some religious order so you can get control of yourself. It makes no sense to invest, make money and blow it. It is the lack of self-discipline that causes most lottery winners to go broke soon after winning millions. It is the lack of self-discipline that causes people who get a raise to immediately go out and buy a new car or take a cruise.

It is difficult to say which of the ten steps is the most important. But of all the steps, this step is probably the most difficult to master if it is not already a part of your makeup. I would venture to say that it is the lack of personal self-discipline that is the No. 1 delineating factor between the rich, the poor and the middle class.

Simply put, people who have low self-esteem and low tolerance for financial pressure can never, and I mean never, be rich. As I have said, a lesson learned from my rich dad was that "the world will push you around." The world pushes people around not because other people are bullies, but because the individual lacks internal control and discipline. People who lack internal fortitude often become victims of those who have self-discipline.

In the entrepreneur classes I teach, I constantly remind people to not focus on their product, service or widget, but to focus on developing management skills. The three most important management skills necessary to start your own business are:

1. Management of cash flow.
2. Management of people.
3. Management of personal time.

I would say, the skills to manage these three apply to anything, not just entrepreneurs. The three matter in the way you live your life as an individual, or as part of a family, a business, a charitable organization, a city or a nation.

Each of these skills is enhanced by the mastery of self discipline. I do not take the saying "pay yourself first" lightly.

The Richest Man in Babylon, by George Classen, is where the statement "pay yourself first" comes from. Millions of copies have been sold. But while millions of people freely repeat that powerful statement, few follow the advice. As I said, financial literacy allows one to read numbers, and numbers tell the story. By looking at a person's income statement and balance sheet, I can readily see if people who spout the words "pay yourself first" actually practice what they preach.

A picture is worth a thousand words. So let's again compare the financial statements of people who pay themselves first against someone who doesn't.

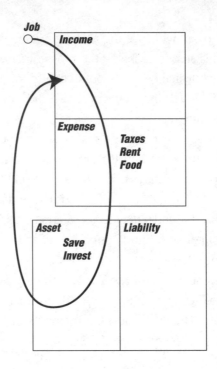

People who pay themselves first

Job

Income	
Expense Taxes Rent Food	
Asset Save Invest	**Liability**

Study the diagrams and notice if you can pick up some distinctions. Again, it has to do with understanding cash flow, which tells the story. Most people look at the numbers and miss the story. If you can truly begin to understand the power of cash flow, you will soon realize what is wrong with the picture on the next page, or why 90 percent of most people work hard all their lives and need government support like Social Security when they are no longer able to work.

Do you see it? The diagram above reflects the actions of an individual who chooses to pay himself first. Each month, they allocate money to their asset column before they pay their monthly expenses. Although millions of people have read Classen's book and understand the words "pay yourself first," in reality they pay themselves last.

Now I can hear the howls from those of you who sincerely believe in paying your bills first. And I can hear all the "responsible" people who pay their bills on time. I am not saying be irresponsible and not pay your bills. All I am saying is do what the book says, which is "pay yourself first." And the diagram above is the correct accounting picture of that action. Not the one that follows.

Someone who pays everyone else first— Often there is nothing left

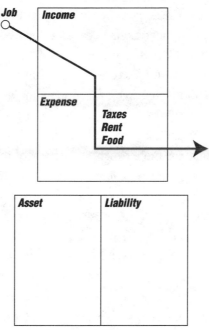

My wife and I have had many bookkeepers and accountants and bankers who have had a major problem with this way of looking at "pay yourself first." The reason is that these financial professionals actually do what the masses do, which is pay themselves last. They pay everyone else first.

There have been months in my life, when for whatever reason, cash flow was far less than my bills. I still paid myself first. My accountant and bookkeeper screamed in panic. "They're going to come after you. The IRS is going to put you in jail." "You're going to ruin your credit rating." "They'll cut off the electricity." I still paid myself first.

"Why?" you ask. Because that's what the story *The Richest Man In Babylon* was all about. The power of self-discipline and the power of internal fortitude. "Guts," in less elegant terms. As my rich dad taught me the first month I worked for him, most people allow the world to push them around. A bill collector calls and you "pay or else." So you pay and not pay yourself. A sales clerk says, "Oh, just put it on your charge card." Your real estate agent tells you to "go ahead—the government allows you a tax deduction on your home." That is what the book is really about. Having the guts to go against the tide and get rich. You may not be weak, but when it comes to money, many people get wimpy.

I am not saying be irresponsible. The reason I don't have high credit card debt, and doodad debt, is because I want to pay myself first. The reason I minimize my income is because I don't want to pay it to the government. That is why, for those of you who have watched the video *The Secrets of the Rich*, my income comes from my asset column, through a Nevada corporation. If I work for money, the government takes it.

Although I pay my bills last, I am financially astute enough to not get into a tough financial situation. I don't like consumer debt. I actually have liabilities that are higher than 99 percent of the population, but I don't pay for them; other people pay for my liabilities. They're called tenants. So rule No. 1 in paying yourself first is don't get into debt in the first place. Although I pay my bills last, I set it up to have only small unimportant bills, that I will have to pay.

Secondly, when I occasionally come up short, I still pay myself first. I let the creditors and even the government scream. I like it when they get tough. Why? Because those guys do me a favor. They inspire me to go out and create more money. So I pay myself first, invest the money, and let the creditors yell. I generally pay them right away anyway. My wife and I have excellent credit. We just don't cave into the pressure and spend our savings or liquidate stocks to pay for consumer debt. That is not too financially intelligent.

So the answer is:

1. Don't get into large debt positions that you have to pay for. Keep your expenses low. Build up assets first. Then, buy the big house or nice car. Being stuck in the rat race is not intelligent.
2. When you come up short, let the pressure build and don't dip into your savings or investments. Use the pressure to inspire your financial genius to come up with new ways of making more money and then pay your bills. You will have increased your ability to make more money as well as your financial intelligence.

So many times I have gotten into financial hot water, and used my brain to create more income, while staunchly defending the assets in my asset column. My bookkeeper has screamed and dived for cover, but I was like a good trooper defending the fort, Fort Assets.

Poor people have poor habits. A common bad habit is innocently called "Dipping into savings." The rich know that savings are only used to create more money, not to pay bills.

I know that sounds tough, but as I said, if you're not tough inside, the world will always push you around anyway.

If you do not like financial pressure, then find a formula that works for you. A good one is to cut expenses, put your money in the bank, pay more than your fair share of income tax, buy safe mutual funds and take the vow of the average. But this violates the "pay yourself first" rule.

The rule does not encourage self-sacrifice or financial abstinence. It doesn't mean pay yourself first and starve. Life was meant to be enjoyed. If you call on your financial genius, you can have all the goodies of life, get rich and pay bills, without sacrificing the good life. And that is financial intelligence.

6. **PAY YOUR BROKERS WELL:** The power of good advice. I often see people posting a sign in front of their house that says, "For Sale by Owner." Or I see on TV today many people claiming to be "Discount Brokers."

My rich dad taught me to take the opposite tack. He believed in paying professionals well, and I have adopted that policy also. Today, I have expensive attorneys, accountants, real estate brokers and stockbrokers. Why? Because if, and I do mean if, the people are professionals, their services should make you money. And the more money they make, the more money I make.

We live in the Information Age. Information is priceless. A good broker should provide you with information as well as take the time to educate you. I have several brokers who are willing to do that for me. Some taught me when I had little or no money, and I am still with them today.

What I pay a broker is tiny in comparison with what kind of money I can make because of the information they provide. I love it when my real estate broker or stockbroker makes a lot of money. Because it usually means I made a lot of money.

A good broker saves me time in addition to making me money—as when I bought the piece of vacant land for $9,000 and sold it immediately for over $25,000, so I could buy my Porsche quicker.

A broker is your eyes and ears to the market. They're there every day so I do not have to be. I'd rather play golf.

Also, people who sell their house on their own must not value their time much. Why would I want to save a few bucks when I could use that time to make more money or spend it with those I love? What I find funny is that so many poor and middle class people insist on tipping restaurant help 15 to 20 percent even for bad service and complain about paying a broker 3 to 7 percent. They enjoy tipping people in the expense column and stiffing people in the asset column. That is not financially intelligent.

All brokers are not created equal. Unfortunately, most brokers are only salespeople. I would say the real estate salespeople are the worst. They sell, but they themselves own little or no real estate. There is a tremendous difference between a broker who sells houses and a broker who sells investments. And that is true for stock, bond, mutual fund and insurance brokers who call themselves financial planners. As in the fairy tale, you kiss a lot of frogs to find one prince. Just remember the old saying, "Never ask an encyclopedia salesperson if you need an encyclopedia."

When I interview any paid professional, I first find out how much property or stocks they personally own and what percentage they pay in taxes. And that applies to my tax attorney as well as my accountant. I have an accountant who minds her own business. Her profession is accounting, but her business is real estate. I used to have an accountant that was a small business accountant, but he had no real estate. I switched because we did not love the same business.

Find a broker who has your best interests at heart. Many brokers will spend the time educating you, and they could be the best asset you find. Just be fair, and most of them will be fair to you. If all you can think about is cutting their commissions, then why should they want to be around you? It's just simple logic.

As I said earlier, one of the management skills is the management of people. Many people only manage people they feel smarter than and they have power over, such as subordinates in a work situation. Many middle managers remain middle managers, failing to get promoted because they know how to work with people below them, but not with people above them. The real skill is to manage and pay well the people who are smarter than you in some technical area. That is why companies have a board of directors. You should have one, too. And that is financial intelligence.

7. **BE AN "INDIAN GIVER":** This is the power of getting something for nothing. When the first white settlers came to America, they

were taken aback by a cultural practice some American Indians had. For example, if a settler was cold, the Indian would give the person a blanket. Mistaking it for a gift, the settler was often offended when the Indian asked for it back.

The Indians also got upset when they realized the settlers did not want to give it back. That is where the term "Indian giver" came from. A simple cultural misunderstanding.

In the world of the "asset column," being an Indian giver is vital to wealth. The sophisticated investor's first question is, "How fast do I get my money back?" They also want to know what they get for free, also called a piece of the action. That is why the ROI, or return of and on investment, is so important.

For example, I found a small condominium, a few blocks from where I live, that was in foreclosure. The bank wanted $60,000, and I submitted a bid for $50,000, which they took, simply because, along with my bid, was a cashier's check for $50,000. They realized I was serious. Most investors would say, aren't you tying up a lot of cash? Would it not be better to get a loan on it? The answer is, not in this case. My investment company uses this as a vacation rental in the winter months, when the "snowbirds" come to Arizona, and rent it for $2,500 a month for four months out of the year. For rental during the off-season, it rents for only $1,000 a month. I had my money back in about three years. Now I own this asset, which pumps money out for me, month in and month out.

The same is done with stocks. Frequently, my broker will call me and recommend I move a sizable amount of money into the stock of a company that he feels is just about to make a move that will add value to the stock, like announcing a new product. I will move my money in for a week to a month while the stock moves up. Then, I pull my initial dollar amount out, and stop worrying about the fluctuations of the market, because my initial money is back and ready to work on another asset. So my money goes in, and then it comes out, and I own an asset that was technically free.

True, I have lost money on many occasions. But I only play with money I can afford to lose. I would say, on an average ten investments, I hit home runs on two or three, while five or six do nothing, and I lose on two or three. But I limit my losses to only the money I have in at that time.

For people who hate risk, they put their money in the bank. And in the long run, savings are better than no savings. But it takes a long time to get your money back and, in most instances, you don't get anything for free with it. They used to hand out toasters, but they rarely do that these days.

On every one of my investments, there must be an upside, something for free. A condominium, a mini-storage, a piece of free land, a house, stock shares, office building. And there must be limited risk, or a low-risk idea. There are books devoted entirely to this subject that I will not get into here. Ray Kroc, of McDonald's fame, sold hamburger franchises, not because he loved hamburgers, but because he wanted the real estate under the franchise for free.

So wise investors must look at more than ROI; it's the assets you get for free once you get your money back. That is financial intelligence.

8. **ASSETS BUY LUXURIES:** The power of focus. A friend's child has been developing a nasty habit of burning a hole in his pocket. Just 16, he naturally wanted his own car. The excuse, "All his friends' parents gave their kids cars." The child wanted to go into his savings and use it for a down payment. That was when his father called me.

"Do you think I should let him do it, or should I just do as other parents do and just buy him a car?"

To which I answered. "It might relieve the pressure in the short term, but what have you taught him in the long term? Can you use this desire to own a car and inspire your son to learn something?" Suddenly the lights went on, and he hurried home.

Two months later I ran into my friend again. "Does your son have his new car?" I asked.

"No, he doesn't. But I went and handed him $3,000 for the car. I told him to use my money instead of his college money."

"Well, that's generous of you," I said.

"Not really. The money came with a hitch. I took your advice of using his strong desire to buy a car and use that energy so he could learn something."

"So what was the hitch?" I asked.

"Well, first we broke out your game again, *CASHFLOW*. We played it and had a long discussion about the wise use of money. I then gave him a subscription to the Wall Street Journal, and a few books on the stock market."

"Then what?" I asked. "What was the catch?"

"I told him the $3,000 was his, but he could not directly buy a car with it. He could use it to buy and sell stocks, find his own stockbroker, and once he had made $6,000 with the $3,000, the money would be his for the car, and the $3,000 would go into his college fund."

"And what are the results?" I asked.

"Well, he got lucky early in his trading, but lost all he gained a few days later. Then, he really got interested. Today, I would say he is down $2,000, but his interest is up. He has read all the books I bought him and he's gone to the library to get more. He reads the Wall Street Journal voraciously, watching for indicators, and he watches CNBC instead of MTV. He's got only $1,000 left, but his interest and learning are sky high. He knows that if he loses that money, he walks for two more years. But he does not seem to care. He even seems uninterested in getting a car because he's found a game that is more fun."

"What happens if he loses all the money?" I asked.

"We'll cross that bridge when we get to it. I'd rather have him lose everything now rather than wait till he's our age to risk losing everything. And besides, that is the best $3,000 I've ever spent on his education. What he is learning will serve him for life, and he seems to have gained a new respect for the power of money. I think he's stopped the burning of holes in his pockets."

As I said in the section "Pay Yourself First," if a person cannot master the power of self-discipline, it is best not to try to get rich. For while the process of developing cash flow from an asset column in theory is easy, it is the mental fortitude of directing money that is hard. Due to external temptations, it is much easier in today's consumer world to simply blow it out the expense column. Because of weak mental fortitude, that money flows into the paths of least resistance. That is the cause of poverty and financial struggle.

I gave this numerical example of financial intelligence, in this case the ability to direct money to make more money.

If we gave 100 people $10,000 at the start of the year, I gave my opinion that at the end of the year:

- 80 would have nothing left. In fact, many would have created greater debt by making a down payment on a new car, refrigerator, TV, VCR or a holiday.
- 16 would have increased that $10,000 by 5 percent to 10 percent.
- 4 would have increased it to $20,000 or into the millions.

We go to school to learn a profession so we can work for money. It is my opinion that it is also important to learn how to have money work for you.

I love my luxuries as much as anyone else. The difference is, some people buy their luxuries on credit. It's the keep-up-with-the-Joneses trap. When I wanted to buy a Porsche, the easy road would have been to call my banker and get a loan. Instead of choosing to focus in the liability column, I chose to focus in the asset column.

As a habit, I used my desire to consume to inspire and motivate my financial genius to invest.

Too often today, we focus to borrowing money to get the things we want instead of focusing on creating money. One is easier in the short term, but harder in the long term. It's a bad habit that we as individuals and as a nation have gotten into. Remember, the easy road often becomes hard, and the hard road often becomes easy.

The earlier you can train yourself and those you love to be masters of money, the better. Money is a powerful force. Unfortunately, people use the power of money against them. If your financial intelligence is low, money will run all over you. It will be smarter than you. If money is smarter than you, you will work for it all your life.

To be the master of money, you need to be smarter than it. Then money will do as it is told. It will obey you. Instead of being a slave to it, you will be the master of it. That is financial intelligence.

9. **THE NEED FOR HEROES:** The power of myth. When I was a kid, I greatly admired Willie Mays, Hank Aaron, Yogi Berra. They were my heroes. As a kid playing Little League, I wanted to be just like them. I treasured their baseball cards. I wanted to know everything about them. I knew the stats, the RBI, the ERAs, their batting averages, how much they got paid, and how they came up from the minors. I wanted to know everything because I wanted to be just like them.

Every time, as a 9 or 10 year-old kid, when I stepped up to bat or played first base or catcher, I wasn't me. I was Yogi or Hank. It's one of the most powerful ways we learn that we often lose as adults. We lose our heroes. We lose our naiveté.

Today, I watch young kids playing basketball near my home. On the court they're not little Johnny; they're Michael Jordan, Sir Charles or Clyde. Copying or emulating heroes is true power learning. And that is why when someone like O.J. Simpson falls from grace, there is such a huge outcry.

There is more than just a courtroom trial. It is the loss of a hero. Someone people grew up with, looked up to, and wanted to be like. Suddenly we need to rid ourselves of that person.

I have new heroes as I grow older. I have golf heroes such as Peter Jacobsen, Fred Couples and Tiger Woods. I copy their swings and do my best to read everything I can about them. I also have heroes such as Donald Trump, Warren Buffett, Peter Lynch, George Soros and Jim Rogers. In my older years, I know their stats just like I knew the ERAs and RBI of my baseball heroes. I follow what Warren Buffett invests in, and read anything I can about his point of view on the market. I read Peter Lynch's book to understand how he chooses stocks. And I read about Donald Trump, trying to find out how he negotiates and puts deals together.

Just as I was not me when I was up to bat, when I'm in the market or I'm negotiating a deal, I am subconsciously acting with the bravado of Trump. Or when analyzing a trend, I look at it as though Peter Lynch were doing it. By having heroes, we tap into a tremendous source of raw genius.

But heroes do more than simply inspire us. Heroes make things look easy. It's the making it look easy that convinces us to want to be just like them. "If they can do it, so can I."

When it comes to investing, too many people make it sound hard. Instead find heroes who make it look easy.

10. **TEACH AND YOU SHALL RECEIVE:** The power of giving. Both of my dads were teachers. My rich dad taught me a lesson I have carried all my life, and that was the necessity of being charitable or giving. My educated dad gave a lot by the way of time and knowledge, but almost never gave away money. As I

said, he usually said that he would give when he had some extra money. Of course, there was rarely any extra.

My rich dad gave money as well as education. He believed firmly in tithing. "If you want something, you first need to give," he would always say. When he was short of money, he simply gave money to his church or to his favorite charity.

If I could leave one single idea with you, it is that idea. Whenever you feel "short" or in "need" of something, give what you want first and it will come back in buckets. That is true for money, a smile, love, friendship. I know it is often the last thing a person may want to do, but it has always worked for me. I just trust that the principle of reciprocity is true, and I give what I want. I want money, so I give money, and it comes back in multiples. I want sales, so I help someone else sell something, and sales come to me. I want contacts and I help someone else get contacts, and like magic, contacts come to me. I heard a saying years ago that went, "God does not need to receive, but humans need to give."

My rich dad would often say, "Poor people are more greedy than rich people." He would explain that if a person was rich, that person was providing something that other people wanted. In my life, over all these years, whenever I have felt needy or short of money or short of help, I simply went out or found in my heart what I wanted, and decided to give it first. And when I gave, it always came back.

It reminds me of the story of the guy sitting with firewood in his arms on a cold freezing night, and he is yelling at the pot-bellied stove, "When you give me some heat, then I'll put some wood in." And when it comes to money, love, happiness, sales and contacts, all one needs to remember is first to give what you want and it will come back in droves. Often just the process of thinking of what I want, and how could I give what I want to someone else, breaks free a torrent of bounty. Whenever I feel that people aren't smiling at me, I simply begin smiling and saying hello, and like magic, there are suddenly more smiling people around me. It is true that your world is only a mirror of you.

So that's why I say, "Teach and you shall receive." I have found that the more I sincerely teach those who want to learn, the more I learn. If you want to learn about money, teach it to someone else. A torrent of new ideas and finer distinctions will come in.

There are times when I have given and nothing has come back or what I have received is not what I wanted. But upon closer inspection and soul searching, I was often giving to receive in those instances, instead of giving to give.

My dad taught teachers, and he became a master teacher. My rich dad always taught young people his way of doing business. In retrospect, it was their generosity with what they knew that made them smarter. There are powers in this world that are much smarter than we are. You can get there on your own, but it's easier with the help of the powers that be. All you need to be is generous with what you have, and the powers will be generous with you.

CHAPTER TEN

Still Want More?
Here are Some
To Do's

*M*any people may not be satisfied with my ten steps. They see them more as philosophies than actions. I think understanding the philosophy is just as important as the action. There are many people who want to do, instead of think, and then there are people who think but do not do. I would say that I am both. I love new ideas and I love action.

So for those who want "to dos" on how to get started, I will share with you some of the things I do, in abbreviated form.

- Stop doing what you're doing. In other words, take a break and assess what is working and what is not working. The definition of insanity is doing the same thing and expecting a different result. Stop doing what is not working and look for something new to do.
- Look for new ideas. For new investing ideas, I go to bookstores and look for books on different and unique subjects. I call them formulas. I buy how-to books on a formula I know nothing about. For example, it was in the bookstore that I found the book *The 16 Percent Solution*, by Joel Moskowitz. I bought the book and read it.

TAKE ACTION! The next Thursday, I did exactly as the book said. Step by step. I have also done that with finding real estate bargains in attorneys' offices and in banks. Most people do not take action, or they let someone talk them out of whatever new formula they are studying. My neighbor told me why 16 percent would not work. I did not listen to him because he's never done it.

- Find someone who has done what you want to do. Take them to lunch. Ask them for tips, for little tricks of the trade. As for 16 percent tax lien certificates, I went to the county tax office and found the government employee who worked in the office. I found out that she, too, invested in the tax liens. Immediately, she was invited to lunch. She was thrilled to tell me everything she knew and how to do it. After lunch, she spent all afternoon showing me everything. By the next day, I found two great properties with her help and have been accruing interest at 16 percent ever since. It took a day to read the book, a day to take action, an hour for lunch, and a day to acquire two great deals.
- Take classes and buy tapes. I search the newspapers for new and interesting classes. Many are for free or a small fee. I also attend and pay for expensive seminars on what I want to learn. I am wealthy and free from needing a job simply because of the courses I took. I have friends who did not take those classes who told me I was wasting my money, and yet they're still at the same job.
- Make lots of offers. When I want a piece of real estate, I look at many properties and generally write an offer. If you don't know what the "right offer" is, neither do I. That is the job of the real estate agent. They make the offers. I do as little work as possible.

A friend wanted me to show her how to buy apartment houses. So one Saturday she, her agent and I went and looked at six apartment houses. Four were dogs, but two were good. I said to write offers on all six, offering half of what the owners asked for. She and the agent nearly had heart attacks. They thought it would be rude, that I might offend the sellers, but I really don't think the agent wanted to work that hard. So they did nothing and went on looking for a better deal.

No offers were ever made, and that person is still looking for the "right" deal at the right price. Well, you don't know what the right price is until you have a second party who wants to deal. Most sellers ask too much. It is rare that a seller will actually ask a price that is less than something is worth.

Moral of the story: Make offers. People who are not investors have no idea what it feels like to be trying to sell something. I have had a piece of real estate that I wanted to sell for months. I would have welcomed anything. I would not care how low the price. They could have offered me ten pigs and I would have been happy. Not at the offer, but just because someone was interested. I would have countered, maybe for a pig farm in exchange. But that's how the game works. The game of buying and selling is fun. Keep that in mind. It's fun and only a game. Make offers. Someone might say "yes."

And I always make offers with escape clauses. In real estate, I make an offer with the words "subject to approval of business partner." I never specify who the business partner is. Most people do not know my partner is my cat. If they accept the offer, and I don't want the deal, I call my home and speak to my cat. I make this absurd statement to illustrate how absurdly easy and simple the game is. So many people make things too difficult and take them too seriously.

Finding a good deal, the right business, the right people, the right investors, or whatever is just like dating. You must go to the market and talk to a lot of people, make a lot of offers, counteroffers, negotiate, reject and accept. I know single people who sit at home and wait for the phone to ring, but unless you're Cindy Crawford or Tom Cruise, I think you'd best go to the market, even if it's only the supermarket. Search, offer, reject, negotiate and accept are all parts of the process of almost everything in life.

- Jog, walk or drive a certain area once a month for ten minutes. I have found some of my best real estate investments while jogging. I will jog a certain neighborhood for a year. What I look for is change. For there to be profit in a deal, there must be two elements: a bargain and change. There are lots of bargains, but it's change that turns a bargain into a profitable opportunity. So when I jog, I jog a neighborhood I might like to invest in. It is the repetition that causes me to notice slight differences. I notice real estate signs that are up for a long time. That means the seller might be more agreeable to deal. I watch for moving trucks, going in or out. I stop and talk to the drivers. I talk to the postal carriers. It's amazing how much information they acquire about an area.

I find a bad area, especially an area that the news has scared everyone away from. I drive it for sometimes a year waiting for signs of something changing for the better. I talk to retailers, especially new ones, and find out why they're moving in. It takes only a few minutes a month, and I do it while doing something else, like exercising, or going to and from the store.

- As for stocks, I like Peter Lynch's book *Beating the Street* for his formula for selecting stocks that grow in value. I have found that the principles of finding value are the same regardless if it's real estate, stocks, mutual funds, new companies, a new pet, a new home, a new spouse, or a bargain on laundry detergent.

The process is always the same. You need to know what you're looking for and then go look for it!

- Why consumers will always be poor. When the supermarket has a sale on, say, toilet paper, the consumer runs in and stocks up. When the stock market has a sale, most often called a crash or correction, the consumer runs away from it. When the supermarket raises its prices, the consumer shops elsewhere. When the stock market raises its prices, the consumer starts buying.

- Look in the right places. A neighbor bought a condominium for $100,000. I bought the identical condo next door to his for $50,000. He told me he's waiting for the price to go up. I told him that his profit is made when you buy, not when you sell. He shopped with a real estate broker who owns no property of her own. I shopped at the foreclosure department of a bank. I paid $500 for a class on how to do this. My neighbor thought that the $500 for a real estate investment class was too expensive. He said he could not afford it, and he couldn't afford the time. So he waits for the price to go up.

- I look for people who want to buy first, then I look for someone who wants to sell. A friend was looking for a certain piece of land. He had the money and did not have the time. I found a large piece of land larger than what my friend wanted to buy, tied it up with an option, called my friend and he wanted a piece of it. So I sold the piece to him and then bought the land. I kept the remaining land as mine for free. Moral of the story: Buy the pie and cut it in pieces. Most people look for what they can afford, so they look too small. They buy only a piece of the pie, so they end up paying more for less. Small thinkers don't get the big breaks. If you want to get richer, think bigger first.

Retailers love giving volume discounts, simply because most business people love big spenders. So even if you're small, you can always think big. When my company was in the market for computers, I called several friends and asked them if they were ready to buy also. We then went to different dealers and negotiated a great deal because we wanted to buy so many. I have done the same with stocks. Small people remain small because they think small; act alone, or don't act all.

- Learn from history. All the big companies on the stock exchange started out as small companies. Colonel Sanders did not get rich until after he lost everything in his 60s. Bill Gates was one of the richest men in the world before he was 30.
- Action always beats inaction.

These are just a few of the things I have done and continue to do to recognize opportunities. The important words being "done" and "do". As repeated many times throughout the book, you must take action before you can receive the financial rewards. Act now!

How To Pay for a Child's College Education for Only $7,000

As the book draws to a close and approaches publication, I would like to share a final thought with you.

The main reason I wrote this book was to share insights into how increased financial intelligence can be used to solve many of life's common problems. Without financial training, we all too often use the standard formulas to get through life, such as to work hard, save, borrow and pay excessive taxes. Today we need better information.

I use the following story as a final example of a financial problem that confronts many young families today. How do you afford a good education for your children and provide for your own retirement? It is an example of using financial intelligence instead of hard work to achieve the same goal.

A friend of mine was griping one day about how hard it was to save money for his four children's college education. He was putting $300 away in a mutual fund each month and had so far accumulated about

$12,000. He estimated he needed $400,000 to get four children through college. He had 12 years to save for it, since his oldest child was then 6 years of age.

The year was 1991, and the real estate market in Phoenix was terrible. People were giving houses away. I suggested to my classmate that he buy a house with some of the money in his mutual fund. The idea intrigued him and we began to discuss the possibility. His primary concern was that he did not have the credit with the bank to buy another house, since he was so over-extended. I assured him that there were other ways to finance a property other than through the bank.

We looked for a house for two weeks, a house that would fit all the criteria we were looking for. There were a lot to choose from, so the shopping was kind of fun. Finally, we found a 3 bedroom 2 bath home in a prime neighborhood. The owner had been downsized and needed to sell that day because he and his family were moving to California where another job waited.

He wanted $102,000, but we offered only $79,000. He took it immediately. The home had on it what is called a non-qualifying loan, which means even a bum without a job could buy it without a banker's approval. The owner owed $72,000 so all my friend had to come up with was $7,000, the difference in price between what was owed and what it sold for. As soon as the owner moved, my friend put the house up for rent. After all expenses were paid, including the mortgage, he put about $125 in his pocket each month.

His plan was to keep the house for 12 years and let the mortgage get paid down faster, by applying the extra $125 to the principle each month. We figured that in 12 years, a large portion of the mortgage would be paid off and he could possibly be clearing $800 a month by the time his first child went to college. He could also sell the house if it had appreciated in value.

In 1994, the real estate market suddenly changed in Phoenix and he was offered $156,000 for the same house by the tenant who lived in it and loved it. Again, he asked me what I thought, and I naturally said sell, on a 1031 tax-deferred exchange.

Suddenly, he had nearly $80,000 to operate with. I called another friend in Austin, Texas who then moved this tax deferred money into a mini-storage facility. Within three months, he began receiving checks for a little less than a $1,000 a month in income which he then poured back into the college mutual fund that was now building much faster. In 1996, the mini-warehouse sold and he received a check for nearly $330,000 as proceeds from the sale which was again rolled into a new project that would now throw off over $3,000 a month in income, again, going into the college mutual fund. He is now very confident that his goal of $400,000 will be met easily, and it only took $7,000 to start and a little financial intelligence. His children will be able to afford the education that they want and he will then use the underlying asset, wrapped in his C Corporation, to pay for his retirement. As a result of this successful investment strategy he will be able to retire early.

Thank you for reading this book. I hope it has provided some insights into utilizing the power of money to work for you. Today, we need greater financial intelligence to simply survive. The idea that it takes money to make money is the thinking of financially unsophisticated people. It does not mean that they're not intelligent. They have simply not learned the science of making money.

Money is only an idea. If you want more money simply change your thinking. Every self-made person started small with an idea, then turned it into something big. The same applies with investing. It takes only a few dollars to start and grow it into something big. I meet so many people who spend their lives chasing the big deal, or trying to mass a lot of money to get into a big deal, but to me that is foolish. Too often I have seen unsophisticated investors put their large nest egg into one deal and lose most of it rapidly. They may have been good workers but they were not good investors.

Education and wisdom about money are important. Start early. Buy a book. Go to a seminar. Practice. Start small. I turned $5,000 cash into a $1 million dollar asset producing $5,000 a month cash flow in less than six years. But I started learning as a kid. I encourage you to learn because it's not that hard. In fact, it's kind of easy once you get the hang of it.

I think I have made my message clear. It's what is in your head that determines what is in your hands. Money is only an idea. There is a great book called *Think and Grow Rich*. The title is not Work Hard and Grow Rich. Learn to have money work hard for you and your life will be easier and happier. Today, don't play it safe, play it smart.

Take Action!

*A*ll of you were given two great gifts: your mind and your time. It is up to you to do what you please with both. With each dollar bill that enters your hand, you and only you have the power to determine your destiny. Spend it foolishly, you choose to be poor. Spend it on liabilities, you join the middle class. Invest it in your mind and learn how to acquire assets and you will be choosing wealth as your goal and your future. The choice is yours and only yours. Every day with every dollar, you decide to be rich, poor or middle class.

Choose to share this knowledge with your children, and you choose to prepare them for the world that awaits. No one else will.

You and your children's future will be determined by choices you make today, not tomorrow.

We wish you great wealth and much happiness with this fabulous gift called life.

Robert Kiyosaki
Sharon Lechter

Robert Kiyosaki's Edumercial

An Educational Commercial

The Three Incomes

In the world of accounting, there are three different types of income. They are:

1. Earned Income
2. Passive Income
3. Portfolio Income

When my real dad said to me, "Go to school, get good grades, and find a safe secure job." he was recommending I work for earned income. When my rich dad said, "The rich don't work for money, they have their money work for them," he was talking about passive income and portfolio income. Passive income, in most cases, is income derived from real estate investments. Portfolio income is income derived from paper assets...paper assets such as stocks, bonds, and mutual funds. Portfolio income is the income that makes Bill Gates the richest man in the world, not earned income.

Rich dad used to say, "The key to becoming wealthy is the ability to convert earned income into passive income and/or portfolio income as quickly as possible." He would say, "The taxes are highest on earned income. The least taxed income is passive income. That is another reason why you want your money working hard for you. The government taxes the income you work hard for more, than the income your money works hard for."

In my second book, *The CASHFLOW Quadrant*, I explain the four different types of people who make up the world of business. They are E- employee, S- self-employed, B- Business Owner and I- Investor. Most people go to school to learn to be an 'E' or 'S'. The *CASHFLOW Quadrant* is written about the *core* differences between the four different people and how people can make a change of quadrant. In fact, most of our products are created for the people in the 'B' and 'I' quadrants.

In *Rich Dad's Guide To Investing*, book #3 in this Rich Dad series, I go into the importance of converting earned income into passive and portfolio income in more detail. Rich dad used to say, "All a real investor does is convert earned income into passive and portfolio income. If you know what you're doing investing is not risky. It's just common sense."

The Key to Financial Freedom

The key to financial freedom and great wealth is a person's ability or skill to convert earned income into passive income and/or portfolio income. That is the skill that my rich dad spent a lot of time teaching Mike and me. Having that skill is the reason my wife Kim and I are financially free, never needing to work again. We continue to work because we choose to. Today we own a real estate investment company for passive income and participate in private placements and initial public offerings of stock for portfolio income.

We also went back to work with our partner Sharon Lechter to build this financial education company to create and publish books, tapes, and games. All of our educational products were created to teach the same skills my rich dad taught me, the skills of converting earned income into passive and portfolio income.

The three board games we created are important because they teach what books cannot teach. For example, you could never learn to ride a bicycle by only reading a book. Our financial education games, *CASHFLOW 101*, which is a sophisticated game for adults, and *CASHFLOW for Kids*, are designed to teach players the basic investment skills' of how to convert earned income into passive income and portfolio income. They also teach the principles of accounting and financial literacy. These games are the only educational products in the world that teach people all of these skills simultaneously.

CASHFLOW 202 is the advanced version of *CASHFLOW 101* and requires the game board from 101, as well as a full understanding of 101, before it can be played. *CASHFLOW 101* and *CASHFLOW* for Kids teach the principles of fundamental investing. *CASHFLOW 202* teaches the principles of technical investing. Technical investing involves advanced trading techniques such as short selling, call options, put options, as well as straddles. A person who understands these advanced techniques is able to make money when the market goes up as well as when the market comes down. As my rich dad would say, "A real investor makes money in an up market and a down market. That is why they make so much money." One of the reasons they make more money is simply because they have more self-confidence. Rich dad would say, "They have more self-confidence because they are less afraid of losing." In other words, the average investor does not make as much money because they are so afraid of losing money. The average investor does not know how to protect themselves from losses, and that is what *CASHFLOW 202* teaches.

The average investor thinks investing is risky because the average investor has not been formally trained to be a professional investor. As Warren Buffet, America's richest investor says, "Risk comes from not knowing what you're doing." My board games teach the simple basics of fundamental investing and technical investing while people are having fun.

I occasionally hear someone say, "Your educational games are expensive." (*CASHFLOW 101* costs $195.00, *CASHFLOW 202* costs $145.00, and *CASHFLOW for Kids* costs $79.00 in the U.S.) All of our game products are complete learning programs and include audio cassettes, videos and/or books. (One reason for our pricing is that we only produce a limited quantity per year.) I nod my head and reply, "Yes they are... especially when compared to entertainment board games." And then silently I say to myself, "But my games are not as expensive as a college education, working hard all your life for earned income, paying excessive taxes, and then living in terror of losing all of your money in the investment markets."

As that occasional person walks away mumbling about the price, I can hear my rich dad saying, "If you want to be rich, you must know what kind of income to work hard for, how to keep it, and how to protect it from loss. That is the key to great wealth." Rich dad would also say, "If you do not know those differences in the three incomes and do not learn the skills on how to acquire and protect those incomes, you will probably spend your life earning less than you could and working harder than you should."

So my poor dad thought a good education, a good job, and years of hard work were all you needed to be successful. My rich dad thought a good education was important, but to him it was also important that Mike and I know the differences in the three incomes and what kind of income to work hard for. To him, that was basic financial education. Knowing the differences in the three incomes and learning the investment skills of how to acquire the different incomes is basic education for anyone who strives to acquire great wealth and achieve financial freedom... a special kind of freedom that only a few will ever know. As rich dad states in lesson #1, "The rich do not work for money. They know how to have money work hard for them." Rich dad said "Earned income is money you work for and passive and portfolio income is money working for you." And knowing that little difference in incomes has been significant in my life. Or as Robert Frost's poem ends by stating, "And that made all the difference."

What is the easiest and best way to learn?

In 1994, after becoming financially free, I was searching for a way to teach others what my rich dad had taught me. You can only learn so much by reading. You cannot learn to ride a bicycle by reading a book. It dawned on me that rich dad taught me through repetition. That is why I began creating educational board games. They are, in my opinion, the easiest and best way to learn rather complex subjects.

CASHFLOW® for KIDS

If you are ready to learn how to acquire more passive and portfolio income, the *CASHFLOW* games can be an important first step. If you are ready to improve your financial education, take the opportunity to try our game products for 90 days risk free. All I ask is that after you purchase the game, you play the game with friends to completion at least six times within those 90 days. If you feel you have not learned anything or the games are too difficult, return the game in good condition and we will be happy to refund your money.

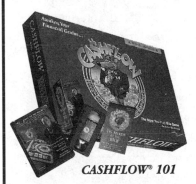

CASHFLOW® 101

It takes playing the games at least 2 times, just to understand the rules and strategies. After the second time the games become easier to play, you will have more fun and your learning will rapidly increase. If you purchase a *CASHFLOW* game and do not play it, it is a very expensive game. If you play it at least 6 times I think you will find each of these games priceless.

CASHFLOW® 202

About the Authors
Robert T. Kiyosaki

"The main reason people struggle financially is because they spent years in school but learned nothing about money. The result is, people learn to work for money... but never learn to have money work for them." says Robert.

Born and raised in Hawaii, Robert is fourth-generation Japanese American. He comes from a prominent family of educators. His father was the head of education for the State of Hawaii. After high school, Robert was educated in New York and upon graduation, he joined the U. S. Marine Corps and went to Vietnam as an officer and a helicopter gunship pilot.

Returning from the war, Robert's business career began. In 1977 he founded a company that brought to the market the first nylon and Velcro "surfer" wallets, which grew into a multi-million dollar worldwide product. He and his products were featured in Runner's World, Gentleman's Quarterly, Success Magazine, Newsweek, and even Playboy.

Leaving the business world, he co-founded in 1985, an international education company that operated in seven countries, teaching business and investing to tens of thousands of graduates.

Retiring at age 47, Robert does what he enjoys most... investing. Concerned about the growing gap between the haves and have nots, Robert created the board game *CASHFLOW*, which teaches the game of money, here before only known by the rich.

Although Robert's business is real estate and developing small cap companies, his true love and passion is teaching. He has shared the speaking stage with such greats as Og Mandino, Zig Ziglar, and Anthony Robbins. Robert Kiyosaki's message is clear. "Take responsibility for your finances or take orders all your life. You're either a master of money or a slave to it." Robert holds classes that last from 1 hour to 3 days teaching people about the secrets of the rich. Although his subjects run from investing for high returns and low risk; to teaching your children to be rich; to starting companies and selling them; he has one solid earth shaking message. And that message is, Awaken The Financial Genius that lies within you. Your genius is waiting to come out.

This is what world famous speaker and author Anthony Robbins says about Robert's work.

"Robert Kiyosaki's work in education is powerful, profound, and life changing. I salute his efforts and recommend him highly."

During this time of great economic change, Robert's message is priceless.

Sharon L. Lechter

Wife and mother of three, CPA, professional manager and consultant to the toy and publishing industries, Sharon Lechter has dedicated her professional efforts to the field of education.

She graduated Summa Cum Laude with a degree in accounting from Florida State University. She went on to be one of the first women to join the ranks of what was then one of the big eight accounting firms, the CFO of a turnaround company in the computer industry, tax director for a national insurance company and founder and Associate Publisher of the first regional woman's magazine in Wisconsin, all the while maintaining her professional credentials as a CPA.

Her focus quickly changed to education as she watched her own three children grow. It was a struggle to get them to read. They would rather watch TV.

So she joined forces with the inventor of the first electronic "talking book" and helped expand the electronic book industry to the multi-million dollar international market it is today. She remains a pioneer in developing new technologies to bring the book back into children's lives.

As her own children grew, she was keenly involved in their education. She became a vocal activist in the areas of mathematics, computers, reading and writing education.

"Our current educational system has not been able to keep pace with the global and technological changes in the world today. We must teach our young people the skills, both scholastic and financial, that they will need not only to survive, but to flourish, in the world they face."

As co-author of *Rich Dad Poor Dad* and the *CASHFLOW Quadrant* she now focuses her efforts in helping to create educational tools for anyone interested in bettering their own financial education.

CASHFLOW Technologies, Inc.

Robert Kiyosaki, Kim Kiyosaki and Sharon Lechter have joined forces as principals of *CASHFLOW Technologies, Inc.* to produce innovative financial education products.

The Company's mission statement reads:
"To elevate the financial well-being of humanity."

CASHFLOW Technologies, Inc. presents Robert's teaching through products such as *Rich Dad Poor Dad, The CASHFLOW Quadrant* and the patented board game *CASHFLOW* (Patent Number 5,826,878), and patent pending board game *CASHFLOW for Kids*. Additional products are available and under development for people searching for financial education to guide them on their path to financial freedom.

Rich Dad Poor Dad is a true story on the lessons about money that Robert Kiyosaki, the author, learned from his two "Dads". One Dad, a PhD and Superintendent of Education never had enough money at the end of the month and died broke. His other Dad dropped out of school at age 13 and went on to become one of the wealthiest men in Hawaii. In *Rich Dad Poor Dad,* Robert explains how to make your money work hard for you instead of you working hard for money. It is available through your local bookstores.

Best-Seller in Australia for over 1 year!

CASHFLOW* ® *Quadrant is the sequel to *Rich Dad Poor Dad.* It's about the four different types of people who make up the world of business: 1) employees, 2) self-employed, 3) business owners and 4) investors and the core value differences between them. It discusses the tools an individual needs to become a successful business owner and investor. It is available through your local bookstores.
Best-Seller in Australia

Rich Dad Poor Dad Part II

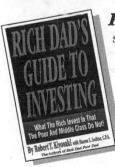

Rich Dad's Guide to Investing is the sequel to *Rich Dad Poor Dad* and the *CASHFLOW Quadrant*. Most of us know that the best investments never make it to market. This book discusses what the rich invest in that the poor and middle class do not. What follows is an insider's look into the world of investing, how the rich find the best investments, and how you can too.

To be released Spring 2000.

*Recommended Reading

For Improving Your Financial Intelligence

As a Man Thinketh, (Inspirational), *James Allen*

Beating the Street (Stock Picking), *Peter Lynch*

Chaos – Making a New Science, (General), *James Gleick*

Creating Wealth (Real Estate), *Robert Allen*

E-Myth (Business), *Michael Gerber*

Incorporate and Grow Rich
(Incorporating) call publisher, Sage Int'l., at 1-800-254-5779, *C.W.Allen*

Investment Biker (Investing), *Jim Rogers*

Market Wizards (Stock Trading), *Jack Schwager*

Over the Top (Success Strategies), *Zig Ziglar*

The New Positioning (Marketing), *Jack Trout*

The Wall Street Journal Guide to Understanding Money & Investing
(Stocks, Bonds, Mutual Funds, Futures, Money),
Kenneth M. Morris , Allan M. Seigel

The Warren Buffet Way (Investment Strategies), *Robert Hagstrom*

Trading For A Living (Stock Trading), *Dr. Alexander Elder*

Trump: The Art of the Deal (Real Estate), *Donald Trump*

Unlimited Power, (Success Strategies), *Anthony Robbins*

Unlimited Wealth (Wealth), *Paul Zane Pilzer*

*These books are suggested readings and may be time sensitive. We always recommend
seeking your own professional, legal, financial and investment advice.

Please visit our website,
www.richdad.com
to review:

- Additional Information About Our Financial Education Products
- Frequently Asked Questions (FAQ's) About Our Products
- Cashflow Technologies Inc.'s Events and Robert Kiyosaki's Appearances and Interviews

Thank You

North America/South America/Europe/Africa:
CASHFLOW™ Technologies, Inc.
4330 N. Civic Center
Scottsdale, Arizona 85251
USA
(480) 998-6971 or (800) 317-3905
Fax: (480) 348-1349
E-Mail: moreinfo@richdad.com

Australia/New Zealand:
CASHFLOW™ Education Australia
Reply Paid AAA401 *(no stamp required)*
PO Box 1126
Crows Nest, NSW 1585, Australia
Tel: (61) 2 9923 1699 or 1 (800) 676-991
Fax: (61) 2 9923 1799 or 1 (800) 676-992
e-mail: info@cashfloweducation.com.au

VISIT OUR WEBSITE: WWW.CASHFLOWTECH.COM